MW01264489

ATTITUDE OF GRACE

JIMMY WILLIAMS

Attitude of Grace

By

Jimmy Williams

ISBN: 979-8-9865413-8-9

Acknowledgments

To my dad, this book would not have been possible without your help. Many nights we sat going over this story while watching a cardinal's game or some golf, followed by hours of your time helping organize what would become Attitude of Grace. We lived it together and we wrote it together.

To Cardinal Glennon Children's Hospital. No words could ever express how much I love this place and all the people in it. From the greatest surgeons in the world, to the army of loving and competent nurses that cared for me. The lady at the Starbucks stand, thanks for loving on my mom throughout our journey, and the ladies in the cafeteria who always had a smile and a joke for my dad. They needed it.

And foremost thank you to my donor's family. Your decision gave me a second chance at life. Someday I will meet Spenser and thank him too.

"He gives strength to the weary and increases the power of the weak. Even youths grow tired and weary, and young men stumble and fall; but those who hope in the LORD will renew their strength. They will soar on wings like eagles; they will run and not grow weary, they will walk and not be faint."

—Isaiah 40:29-31

Foreword

By Jim Williams (Dad)

—~~—

I have had the incredible privilege of having a front-row seat to Jimmy's life. For thirty-nine years, I have been a father. Raising children has filled my life with love, laughter, and occasionally heartache.

From a very early age, Jimmy was often described as an old soul. His mature outlook and demeanor, his warmth, and his maturity only occasionally let through glimpses of childlike behaviors. This might have been a reason for some concern, but the smile that lives on his face nearly every waking moment has given us all great comfort.

Jimmy's sisters were grown and living on their own before he was born, so in many ways, he has lived the life of an only child; his oldest sister, Ashley, got married the same week he was born; his other sister, Whitney, was his nanny for the first few years of his life. The three of them share a special bond; they interact like any other siblings, but his older sisters look up to him in many ways.

Shortly after Jimmy had his heart transplant, Ashley confronted the family about getting regular routine physicals. Our family had been healthy, active people and not prone to getting annual checkups. Upon returning to Tennessee, Ashley lived up to her end of the deal and went to the doctor. Bloodwork revealed a problem. Ashley had myelofibrosis, a rare form of blood cancer that if left unchecked would very likely have taken her life. Ashley has responded well to chemo treatments and is able to carry on with her busy and active life, knowing at some point she will require a bone marrow transplant. She credits Jimmy with saving her life.

Jimmy's story is not just the story about a child having a life-threatening illness; those occur way too often. His story is about a little boy who was prepared.

I cannot and do not believe God did this to Jimmy. I do believe that God knew Jimmy even before he was born. God knew to put so many people in Jimmy's life to help prepare him—not just me as his dad or his mom and sisters but everyone who has touched Jimmy's life, and there are many.

Faith has been a part of his life from a very early age. Constant, secure, and unwavering.

His faith has helped him create this attitude of grace.

From the first IV that went into his arm in the hospital to all the multitude of painful procedures that he has had to endure, he has never complained, has always taken each step with a positive and enduring temperament.

From the time he left the hospital, Jimmy has been constantly engaged in charitable work for Cardinal Glennon Children's Hospital, from raising money through his special appearances at fundraising golf tournaments, where he has a tent set up at a particular hole and sells tee shots, to a toy drive he calls "Jimmy's birthday wish," which is that "every kid at Cardinal Glennon gets a toy." He has delivered over a thousand toys to the hospital. For the 2022 and 2023 baseball season, Jimmy has been the patient cochair for Homers for Health, a program where the St. Louis Cardinals baseball team and Cardinal Hall of Famer Matt Holliday have raised millions of dollars for Cardinal Glennon.

At twelve Jimmy was asked to speak at Holliday's Heroes, a banquet honoring the donors to Homers for Health. Shortly afterward he decided to become a motivational speaker and has shared his story many times to many audiences. Those appearances are what inspired him to write a book and share his story with the world.

How Did We Get Here?

—~~—

Alarms are going off. The glass walls of my room are thrown aside as doctors and nurses rush in. Bri stands over me; her face is just inches from mine as she looks me in the eye and asks if I can feel my heart beating.

"Yes, ma'am, it's beating really fast."

I try to stay as calm and focused as she is. I can see that behind her, they are preparing syringes and paddles to shock my heart. They are all talking, and Bri has a needle stuck into one of my IV lines.

I hear a man ask, "Who did that?"

Bri answers, "I did."

Mom and Dad are standing now, and I can feel Mom praying.

I want to tell them it's going to be OK; I just need to know how I can help.

I am not afraid.

Where I Belong

—∞—

"Hey, is my bike in there?"

The movers—big guys, sweating like crazy—are moving our furniture into our new house in Jackson, my dad's hometown.

Last fall, Dad took me to a high school football game. Jackson is a football town; it seems like the whole town comes to Friday night football. We sat there watching the game with his friends—the same guys he once played football with on that same field. Listening to him and his buddies talk about the old days, I could almost visualize him out there on the field. When the game ended, they had something they wanted to show me, so we walked over to the old gym. The sidewalk in front of the gym was brick. People had their names and the year they went to school on the bricks. OK, kind of cool, I guess. As we approached the main entrance, I saw it.

My dad and his teammate's names were laid out by position in brick. The football team and, next to it, the wrestling team. Dad pointed to his name. I stared for a minute. "Jimmy Williams" right there in brick. That's my name, the same as my dad's. I had a sense of belonging at that moment. Me and Dad needed to talk.

"Dad, I want to live here, go to school where you went to school. Play football on the same field where you played. This is where I belong," I said.

Dad was quiet for a minute. "Son, that's a big request. We have a life in Tennessee, my business, everything," he replied.

"Dad, it's the right thing to do," I said.

—∞—

Now I just want to get my bike out of the back of this moving truck.

"Hey, Dad, can you see if my bike is in there?" I ask.

"Son, what's the big hurry?" Dad replies.

"Dad, I need my bike. I want to go meet all our neighbors," I say.

"Son, there must be one hundred houses in this neighborhood. You think you're going to hit them all?" Dad asks.

"I don't know, maybe," I say.

The man unloading the truck can hear us talking.

He says, "Hey, kid. I'll dig through to the back and get your bike."

They all laugh at the thought of me riding door to door.

He wheels the bike down the truck's wooden ramp, and I am off. I knock on almost every door in the neighborhood and introduce myself.

"Hi, I'm Jimmy Williams. I'm seven years old and just moved in."

I want to meet some kids. There are basketball nets in the driveways, so there must be some kids here. Most of the people I meet are old, like my dad. But I don't give up. I keep knocking on doors.

It's summer, and my baseball season ended before our move. So I'm ready to play some golf. Dad's loading our golf clubs in his truck. There are boxes stacked everywhere in our new house, and Mom stands in the kitchen as me and my dad head out the door.

She looks at Dad and says, "Where you guys headed? We have a ton of unpacking to do."

She acts frustrated with us but just shrugs it off and says, "Go have fun."

We have already joined a golf club in town: Kimbeland Country Club. It's where all my dad's friends play. All we talked about on the trip to Jackson was how we would play golf every day. Dad retired when we moved—no more waiting for him to get home from work or return from a work trip.

I want to play all the sports my dad played. I'm going to be a pro. At what? I haven't decided yet—football, baseball, or both. Dad and I throw a ball every day in the front yard, but he gets worn out quickly. Me? I want to play every minute. Luckily, the golf course has carts.

Golf fills our days. Dad can only throw a ball for about thirty minutes. But he can drive a golf cart all day.

It's getting dark. I'm on the driving range, hitting balls. We've been at the golf course all day. Played eighteen holes. Had lunch. Played eighteen more. My hands hurt. Blisters have torn, and I am bleeding. Dad pulls up in his cart to get me. I walk to the cart and show him my hands.

"Son, you've had enough for today. Mom's going to kill us both," he says.

I reply, "No, Dad, please. Just tape up my hands. I don't want to quit."

Dad gets the white tape out of his bag and tapes up my fingers. He keeps saying, "Jimmy, your mom is going to kill me for this."

This becomes our life. Every morning, we get up early and head to the golf course.

Dad tells my mom, "We are living the dream."

I'm getting better all the time. At first, I tee off from the 150-yard marker on every hole. But as I am able to score par, Dad moves me back to a longer distance. I want to hit from a tee box, but he won't let me until I can par the hole from the shorter distances.

Life is good. My elementary school is close to our house. Mom takes me to school, and most days, Dad picks me up so we can head to the golf course.

Life is not all golf, though. I play baseball in the spring at Jackson City Park, the same field Dad played on when he was a kid. I pitch, and I love it. I make the all-star team.

In the fall I sign up for a tackle football league, and I am so excited. Mom's scared; she thinks I'm too small. But I cannot wait to get those pads on and hit someone. The season starts, and I make a new friend, Jordan. His dad is our coach and quickly moves me to quarterback. I can handle the snap better than most of the kids because I know I'm going to get hit, but I have a job to do, and there ain't nothing going to keep me from getting that ball to Jordan. We quickly become an unstoppable pair. We win every game. I love me some football.

Everything in my life is coming together.

Moving to Jackson is everything I had hoped it would be. A real sports-loving town. Our house is five minutes from my grandparents' house, so I visit them a lot. I miss my sisters. They still live in Tennessee. Ashley is the oldest. She has always seemed more like a second mom—I guess because she has been one for as long as I can remember. My nephew, Jack, is three years younger than me, and his sister, Kate (my niece), is six years younger than me. Jack loves sports as much as I do. They are all huge Tennessee Vols fans. My other sister, Whitney, is married and has a baby girl, Fay. Whitney was my nanny for several years when I was really little. When we are together, we go at it—lots of banter, lots of laughs. I love them. Someday when I am older, I will probably return to live in Tennessee. But for now, I got things to do.

Two years have passed since we moved. My mom takes me to church on Sundays and stays on top of my schoolwork. She is almost as obsessed with those things as my dad is about sports and my future.

When I was six years old, I got baptized. I already understood I wanted to be a Christian and live a faithful life. The day before the baptism, I told my mom I wanted a full immersion.

"Seriously?" she asked.

"Yes," I told her.

I wanted to make sure they baptized me properly—no sprinkles or half dunks for me.

I want all of it. I know who I want to be. I want to do everything I need to live a great life when I get older.

It is our morning round, and Dad is talking about my grip on the club. I guess I express some frustration. As he pulls up to my ball and stops the cart, he tells me to stay put for a second. Another talk. We have lots of them.

"Son, you need to help me here. You play lots of sports. Football, baseball, you're wrestling now, and golf. Not everything needs to be serious business. If you want to play golf for fun, take it casual. That's perfectly fine with me, and I won't care about your swing or grip or anything else. We can relax and play and enjoy our day," he says.

I take my time answering. It matters, and I understand where he is coming from. My golf game has been getting better—a lot better—and I really love it.

"Dad, I really think this can turn into something. I want to take golf seriously. I want to be great. Whatever it takes," I reply.

That day, for the first time, I beat my dad.

My dad knows nothing about junior golf tournaments. He asks around and hears that Jack Connell, the golf pro at Dalhousie Golf Club, is the junior golf director. Dalhousie is in a neighboring town about ten minutes away. At dinner that night, we discuss what we need to do to take my golf game to the next level. We need to see where I stack up against other kids my age that are serious golfers. Dad feels we could use a second place to play, that great golf courses help produce great golfers. The next day we join Dalhousie Golf Club.

As we drive into the parking lot, I can tell we are at a different type of place. Some teenage boys stand by the carts at a place called the bag drop. As we pull up, one of them comes to get our golf clubs and load them on a cart for us.

An older gentleman sits in a golf cart talking to the boys. He gets out of his cart and walks up to me and my dad.

He reaches out to shake my dad's hand and says, "You must be the Williamses. I'm Jack Connell."

Jack tells us all about Dalhousie. A friendship begins that day between the three of us that none of us could see coming.

As Jack shows us around the facility, my dad tells him I am interested in playing in some junior golf tournaments, and we understand he is the guy in charge of our area. Jack hesitates as he looks at me and then my dad.

"Well, Dad, he's pretty little. How old?" Jack asks.

"He's nine," Dad responds.

"Well, Dad, he's kind of small; my youngest age group is eleven and under. He would need to carry his own bag, play his own ball, and keep his own score. I don't allow dads to caddie or help. But I normally leave the final decision up to the parents," Jack says.

Jack points us in the direction of the first tee box, and we drive off.

The course is beautiful. Everything is perfect. The grass

on the tee box looks like a putting green. The fairways look immaculate. Tall native grass lines the fairways, and sand bunkers surround the greens. It looks like a pro course on TV. It looks hard too.

I am small for my age, so I do not hit long, towering drives. But I rarely miss the middle of the fairway. I have good fundamentals, and Dad and I always talk rhythm. Sweep the ball off the tee; don't hit at it. The course looks difficult, but if I stay in the middle of the fairway, all those hazards are nothing more than decoration.

After playing a few holes, we see Jack again. He has been following us from a distance, and we have no idea we are being watched.

As we walk from the tee box on the fourth hole to return to our cart, Jack pulls up and is all smiles. He pulls his cart up beside ours and smiles at my dad as he hands him a sign-up sheet.

"Yeah, he can play and won't have any problem, but I will have some eleven-year-olds that are going to be really disappointed," he says.

I love hearing him say that, and it boosts my confidence, but three weeks is not much time. It is dark before we leave.

It's Dalhousie in the mornings and Kimbeland in the afternoons. And sometimes back to Dalhousie in the evenings.

Dad finds us a hole somewhere in a shaded area, and I practice till it is too dark to see.

—∾—

When we arrive at Hidden Trails Country Club, I see kids everywhere. Golf clubs in pull carts being wheeled through the parking lot. Kids hitting balls on the range and putting on the practice green. My mom is a nervous wreck. Of course, she has always been a nervous wreck at every sport I've played. We unload my clubs, and I head for the range. Dad goes and gets my scorecard and pairings. I will play with a boy from Dexter and a boy from Poplar Bluff. They are both a good bit bigger than me. As we approach the first tee, I strike up a conversation. It helps my nerves. I like to talk about anything, but talking about football is all the better. The parents all ride along in golf carts, looking scared to death. Hey, it ain't football—no one's gonna get crushed.

First tee shot. Down the middle. My distance is almost as good as that of the other boys, and I'm straight. Every shot is down the middle; I'm in the lead after a few holes. I don't know what the other kids my age are shooting, but I am beating the kids in my group.

As we approach the final hole, I can see some other kids waiting around the green. Parents are discussing scores. They are aware I am the lowest so far. The last hole is a par four. I am barely short of the green in two strokes, and a bogey will win the tournament. All I need to do is chip onto the green safely and two-putt for the victory. I chip the ball, and it rolls in the cup. Birdie. I can hear my mom screaming from the parking lot.

My first tournament. My first win. Hats off and shake hands. Congratulate your opponents and go get the medal.

Now I know this is my thing. Jack hands out the medals, and as he puts mine around my neck, he whispers, "Little Jimmy, going to be a lot more where this came from."

And he is right. The spark I had when I started golf has become a raging fire. I play ten tournaments in a row, and they are all wins.

I dream of being on the PGA Tour.

Living the dream

Driving to Jackson and excited to see my new home.

I love football

Wrestling is a family tradition

Jack Connell

Titleist
Titleist

First day at Dalhousie Golf Club.

Grace

—~~—

SPEND AN HOUR WITH JACK, and you know he is a Christian.

He's been teaching golf for forty years and loves to talk, especially about grace.

"Give yourself some grace, Jimmy. Don't let that devil get in your head. If you make a bad shot, shrug it off," he says.

God uses Jack and his golf knowledge as a tool for witnessing his grace. Together they make a great team; I don't know if I will ever be a golf pro, but I know I want to be on their team.

—~~—

Now golf life is not all just fun. One day my dad picks me up from school, and we head for the golf course. We are on the fourth hole at Kimbeland. It's a short downhill par three, and I'm even par through the first three holes.

I hit a great approach shot onto the green, leaving me about an eight-foot putt left for a birdie. I'm already beating my dad by a stroke; a birdie here, and I can start talking some smack.

I putt the ball—it heads straight for the cup. I've read the putt perfectly; speed is perfect, and right before it gets to the hole, it hops, catches the side of the cup, and lips out.

I am so mad, like furious. I stomp off the green, kick the cart, and slam my putter on the ground. My mom would not like the language coming out of my mouth either.

Dad drives up to the next tee box and gets out of the cart, but instead of getting his driver out of his bag, he takes my bag off the back of the cart. I think, "Oh no, this ain't good."

Dad takes my bag of clubs, walks over by the trees, and throws my entire bag into the woods.

Now I am panicking. I cry before my dad ever says a word.

"Son, with an attitude like that, you don't deserve those clubs. That's life. You get a bad break; you suck it up and move on. You don't throw fits," he says.

Dad never gets mad about a bad shot or a missed putt. But let my attitude slip? Boom.

I get it. If you want to be a great athlete, you need a great attitude.

I don't get those clubs back till the end of the round.

Tournaments, PB&Js, and Nausea

TWENTY NINETEEN. SUMMER HAS COME, and I've just finished fourth grade. I'm ready for a summer of travel baseball. (And yes, another summer of golf tournaments). But something is different. Our normal routine is to arrive at the golf course around 8:00 a.m. We hit some balls on the range, chip, and putt for about an hour of practice before heading out to the first tee. But today, I'm tired, and we haven't even started yet. I hit a few, grab a bottle of water at the food pavilion near the practice area, and sit in the cart.

Dad walks over to the cart. "Son, is everything OK?" he asks.

"Sure, Dad, I'm not feeling great. Can we skip the range and go play?" I ask.

He shrugs it off, and we head out to the course. This starts to happen a lot. I'm nauseous and tired. It's not terrible, but something is wrong. I wish I could feel like I used to.

Mom's worried, and the doctor's appointments begin.

My parents are both on me hard about the foods I eat, so I'm trying to do better. But when you don't feel good, you sure don't want to eat something you don't like.

In June, the golf tournaments begin, and I'm winning. I can sense that I've built a reputation in our little golf world for being a great golfer and a hard worker.

The other kids know I'm always the favorite to win, and I love that. But as much as I love golf, I'm not begging to stay at the course all day. These days I'm done with one round and going to the range is rare.

Dad is concerned, and Mom is worried. Am I not feeling good, or am I getting burned out?

We have a long talk. It bothers me that they think I don't want to play. My energy is not the same, and I am trying to eat better but not doing a very good job.

My dad and I plan a golf trip. We are going to travel through Ohio, Kentucky, and Tennessee. Play a different course every day. If we think I'm up to it when we're done, we will travel to Orlando on the first of August for the Hurricane Junior World Championships.

We're convinced it's time for me to compete against the best players we can find.

We play some great courses. The last stop on our trip is the Legends Golf Club. I shoot a seventy-six and crush my dad. I tell him I'm ready; let's book Orlando.

August 3. Orange County National Golf Complex in Orlando. It's an intimidating place. It's *huge*. There are multiple courses and hundreds of kids from all over the world.

It's day one of a three-day tournament. It's one hundred degrees, and I feel nauseous. I'm coming to terms with it. I guess this is going to be my normal. I need to push through. I'm playing fair. Not great, just fair.

Day two. I'm putting on the practice green before my round starts. As I come off the green, I throw up.

My parents think I need to quit.

"Let's go back to the room. Take it easy," Mom says.

They know I'm not going to quit. There is no way. I get through the round, and I'm exhausted.

The third and final round comes. I would normally spend an hour hitting balls, chipping, and putting. But not today. I take a few minutes on the putting green but skip the practice range to conserve my energy; it's 9:00 a.m. and already hot.

It seems like every hole is uphill. Walking for the next five hours will take all there is in me. I tell my parents I'm fine, but I'm not.

I start in fifth place. That's not bad, but fifth place doesn't get a trophy. This is by far the biggest tournament of my life, and I really want a trophy.

The goal today is to get through the tournament. I'm paired with a kid from Peru. He seems like a great kid, so I try to chat it up with him, but he doesn't speak great English. We talk some but not a lot.

The Hurricane tournament allows us to use caddies, so my dad is on the bag for me. As far as dad caddies go, he is pretty hands off. He has the clubs and gets me yardages sometimes, but that's about it. I prefer to do everything myself, but today I am really thankful he is here and carrying the bag.

The first hole is a long par five. It's a dogleg right and uphill all the way to the green. I catch my driver flush, and it goes dead straight. Right down the middle, but it stops about twenty-five or thirty yards short of where I have landed the last couple of days. I'm getting weaker, so I really need my short game working today, or it could get embarrassing. Gaining on the other players and tracking the leaderboard is not likely today. I focus on the kid I'm paired with. Beat him if I can, make it through the round.

The round crawls, and it seems like we've been out in the heat all day. My score is not that bad, and as we approach the fifteenth tee box, I decide to check the scoring device they give us. These devices look like a phone; you enter your scores on them and can check the leaderboard. I haven't had the guts till now to even look at where I stand.

I am tied for third place with the kid I am paired with. Immediately, the nerves start. I walk to the back of the tee box where my dad stands by the bag to tell him where we are. He smiles and looks at me with my driver in his hand. He hands me my club and says, "You got this."

For the next three holes, I need to forget how tired I am, stay focused, and play it safe. Let the other guy make a mistake. I'm not sure he knows, and I don't want to be the only one under all this pressure.

I tee off first. There are bunkers everywhere on the course, and this hole has sand bunkers splitting the middle of the fairway. I can't hit it far enough to clear them, and they stretch out for fifty yards, so the fairway available is really tight. I hit a low driver shot with a little left-to-right fade to it. It runs out right beside the sand traps and is safe.

Now before the other kid tees off, I want him to be aware he's tied for third too. So, as I pick up my tee, I casually mention, "Hey, did you know we are tied for third place?" He looks really surprised and walks over to his dad, who is also caddying for him. They take out their scoring device. Wide eyed, he looks up at his dad. I can't tell what they are saying, but the look in that kid's eye lets me know he's feeling some pressure too.

Now as he tees up his driver, those bunkers get wider and longer, as they did for me. In golf, when you're more focused on not hitting your ball into a hazard than hitting your target, you're in trouble. Sure enough, his tee shot finds the middle of that long bunker. I have an edge now. He takes a bogey, and I gain a stroke on the hole. Now all I need to do is stay with him for two holes. We both bogey the seventeenth hole.

On the eighteenth hole, I make par, and it's over. I pull out a third-place finish. My dad is standing off to the side of the green with my golf bag. As I walk up to him with my putter still in hand, he opens his arms, and I practically fall into them. My mom has been following along in a golf cart. Of course, she is in tears.

The trophy ceremony and pictures take a while. It is unbelievable standing there getting pictures taken of me holding my trophy. I smile ear to ear, wanting to take it all in. As Dad finally loads the clubs in the back of the car, I want to get to the room. We get to our hotel, and I crawl into bed, exhausted—done.

On the long drive back to Missouri, I sleep.

As soon as we get settled in at home, Mom gets me a doctor's appointment. Then another and another.

My parents are getting more concerned. I'm not eating or drinking and begin sleeping in their bed. Finally, one morning they take me to the emergency room.

The doctor makes us an appointment at Cardinal

Glennon Children's Hospital in St. Louis to visit a stomach doctor.

I am too sick to even think about it. I really want this to stop. It has been so long since I have felt good that I can't remember what good feels like.

3rd place finish. On top of the world right before everything falls apart

The boy from Peru

Jimmy in the Rough

AUGUST 23. WE MAKE THE two-hour drive to Cardinal Glennon Children's Hospital. The waiting area is full of kids with their parents, but we don't have to wait very long. We are taken back through a door and down a hall to a small room with a bed, just like at the doctor's office. A nurse wraps my arm with the blood pressure cuff and pumps it, air squeezing my arm. As she finishes up, a male doctor comes into our room, sits on a stool, and starts talking to my parents. There is a computer on the desk behind him, and he occasionally turns around and types on it. He feels around on my stomach, puts a stethoscope on my bare chest, and listens to my heart.

I have been to plenty of doctor's appointments by this point, and every visit seems about the same. I just hope this doctor has some medicine that will make the nausea go away.

The doctor tells me he wants to get some pictures of my stomach while my mom and dad wait in the room. We all believe that I will be right back. I'm not too nervous. The great thing about X-rays is that they don't hurt; they're just pictures. They will lay me down, snap the pictures, sit me up, snap more pictures, and that will be it. No big deal. I think, "Well, this is going to work. They'll see what's wrong with my stomach, get me some medicine, and we'll be headed home." I am wrong.

I'm not in the X-ray room long before a different nurse shows up, puts me back in the wheelchair, and down the hall we go. We're headed in a different direction. As we approach the elevator, the nurse tells me she is taking me to a different room; my parents will be along shortly. We get on the elevator and head to the second floor. I'm still not nervous, but as we get off the elevator and pass through some wide double doors, I realize we are in an entirely different part of the hospital. We approach what seems to be a large reception desk. People are busy going back and forth. The hallway is lined with rooms that have glass walls and doors. We turn left into one of the rooms, where a lady is waiting for me. She is a nurse and lets me know my parents are on their way.

"Where am I?" I ask.

"Honey, you're in the PICU. My name is Mary Grace, and I will be taking care of you." She smiles.

She looks like a very nice person; she has brown hair, smiles a lot, and has a confident way about her that reminds me of a schoolteacher.

While I am being moved to the PICU, my parents are taken to a room where some doctors are waiting for them. In that room, they have been told that the problem is not my stomach but my heart. I have pediatric dilated cardiomyopathy. My heart is failing. I have 17 percent heart function and am fighting for my life.

"Hey, buddy." I hear my dad's voice as he and my mom walk into my room.

Mom does the mom thing and heads straight for me. She leans in and starts hugging and kissing me. Dad reaches over and takes my hand.

The nurse gives me a hospital gown, which I change into before crawling up into the bed.

Out comes the first needle; it isn't too bad. She puts the needle inside my left arm, right where it bends. Now there is a needle in my arm with tape holding it in place and a plastic line running up beside me to an IV. She says I am dehydrated and they just need to get some liquids in me.

The room has a couch along the wall with a window and some small cabinets in the corner. I have a TV on the wall across from my bed. I can see through the glass walls to the hallway and the reception area.

I look at my mom and ask her what's going on. She looks at my dad. He's still holding my hand and says, "Well, it turns out that your heart is not doing really good. And it's been the cause of your stomach feeling sick."

I really don't know what to think. I just close my eyes for a second and look back at Dad.

"My heart?" I ask.

Mary Grace stands by my bed.

"Jimmy, when your heart has trouble getting blood to all the parts of your body that it needs to, it starts to pick where it needs the blood to go the most and then stops sending as much to other places. Like the stomach. So that's why you started feeling sick," she says.

So, it's real. I'm sick. There is a reason why I have been feeling this way.

Everybody has been sick. Nauseous. Sometimes it's like only half your stomach feels sick; it grows till it's just too much, and then you throw up. We've all had that. But it usually goes away in a day or two. I have felt "half sick" every day for so long that I can't remember when it started. When I'm nauseous, I don't have energy and feel weak.

When these feelings didn't go away, I tried to ignore them and kept doing the things I wanted to do. Sometimes the feelings got worse, and I would throw up; but instead of feeling better, I went back to feeling half sick.

Now I know it's real. I am sick for a reason, and it's not my fault.

I can't remember the last time I was hungry. Mom tells the nurses I have not eaten or drunk much for about four days.

The nurse asks me what I would like to drink and if I want to order some food. I shake my head no. I just can't. I don't have the energy to force myself, and I am more than half sick.

There is a couch at the far end of the room by the window. Mom and Dad take their places on it while more doctors and nurses come in and out of the room. I lay my head back on the pillow; I'm worn out. I close my eyes part of the time. I can't sleep, so I just try to listen.

Mary Grace tells me she needs to put in another IV. I hear her telling the other nurse that my veins are difficult to stick—probably because I am so dehydrated. She gets it first try. That would not always be the case.

There are people in and out; it's getting late. A new doctor comes up to my bed to talk to me. She's a good bit older than the nurses and doctors who have been in and out so far. She might even be older than my dad. She's not very tall and thin.

"Hello, Jimmy. I am Dr. Andreone," she says.

I take it that she is the boss in the PICU; she just seems like someone in charge. She becomes a fixture outside my room.

Two nurses are now in my room full time. There is a computer on a stand with wheels at the bottom so they can push it around. One of the nurses is always typing on it. There are computer monitors with a bunch of stuff on them attached to a wall. My heartbeat shows on them. The tall shiny pole holding the IV now has an electronic device just below the bag. The plastic lines run through it, and it beeps loudly when it's time to add more drugs.

The room is plain: green floor, light-yellow walls, and a white ceiling. My glass sliding door is closed now, and a curtain has been slid across the glass wall facing the hallway. It's dark outside.

I ask Mom, "How long am I going to be here?"

"Well, Jimmy, I don't know for sure. Hopefully not too long, babe, just till you get better," she says.

"Hey, Dad, can you turn the TV on and find ESPN?" I ask.

It's been a long day. I don't like what's happening. I feel even worse than I did yesterday. I close my eyes and go to sleep.

This is the first time I have been in the hospital overnight.

I don't sleep—maybe in pieces but not regular sleep. They just keep coming: doctors, nurses, and now Mike.

Mike is pushing a big computer screen on a cart. He comes in and sits down beside me.

"Hey, I'm Mike. I'm going to take an echo of your heart," he says.

I ask what that is, and he describes it in detail. Now me and Mike will have a lot of these visits, and there is no one I enjoy hanging out with more. He loves football. We banter the entire time, and he learns I like the Georgia Bulldogs. An hour after he leaves, a Georgia Bulldogs football is delivered to my room.

The first twenty-four hours are busy. More IVs are added, and my heart rate and blood pressure are constantly monitored. I can't eat and get sick between a few sips of Sprite.

The blood pressure cuff keeps inflating on its own; every few minutes, it squeezes me and reports my blood pressure to the computer screen. Stickers all over my chest report my heartbeat. When I can get the energy, I ask questions: What's this? What's that? What's it for?

My nurses tell me anything I want to know. Mary Grace has a conversation with my dad about it, and they agree: tell me whatever I want to know.

I don't want a bunch of secrets.

Eventually, my veins become exhausted, partly from

dehydration but also from the trauma of being stuck over and over. Adding an IV takes more than one try. Sometimes they blow through the vein: the needle goes in and out the other side. Sometimes the vein rolls over, and they can't get the needle in it. Man, it hurts when they have that needle in you, digging and digging to get in the vein.

I don't want to be a problem. I am grateful for all these people who are really trying to help me. I know it in my heart, so I don't complain when it hurts.

The nurse always says, "Oh, Jimmy, I'm so sorry."

I just say, "It's OK."

—∞—

It's been about three days, and I am learning the routine here. It's 6:00 a.m., and a group of doctors and nurses stand outside my room—this happens at least twice a day, in the morning and evening. My dad and I are always awake early. I can see the doctors and nurses through the glass walls, but I want to hear what they are saying, so I ask my dad to open the doors and pull back the curtains. It is still difficult to take in what they are talking about, so I ask the nurse to put me in a wheelchair and get me closer to them. They pause their discussion long enough for me to get situated; there are a few smiles at the notion that a kid wants in on the conversation.

Now I can hear what medications I will get today. I learn which ones get pushed through with a needle, which ones ache as they go in, and which ones burn. I just want to understand and get my mind right.

Everyone listens to a gray-haired doctor standing in the middle of the group. He talks in a real serious manner, asking several of the younger doctors questions about my blood work and echo results. He asks my nurse about anything that went on during the night.

He walks into my room and introduces himself.

"Hello, Jimmy, I am Dr. Huddleston," he says.

I know he is important immediately. He is making the decisions. He decides what happens to me.

We have a conversation about me. We talk about what sports I've played, football and golf. He tries to figure me out. I try to figure him out too. I realize I am a very sick kid. Lying in this bed, I am pretty much skin and bones. My eyes are sunk back with dark circles around them, but I want him to know I am an athlete. This is not the real me. I don't want him to think I have always been like this. They need to know what I am supposed to be like so they can get me back to the real me.

Dr. Huddleston starts talking to my dad, asking him to pull up videos of me running and playing baseball and football on his phone. I know he is searching for something; I just don't know what.

Later they will run a series of tests for muscular dystrophy, which can sometimes cause my heart condition.

He asks what I've had to eat. He will ask me that a hundred times over the coming weeks.

"Got to get some food in this kid," he says.

The group is at my door every day at 6:00 a.m. and 6:00 p.m. Dr. Huddleston, his partner, Dr. Fiore, and at least six or seven more doctors gather every time I get pulled up to the door. I listen to all of them, but I never take my eyes off Dr. Huddleston. I know somehow that my life is in his hands. Both he and Dr. Fiore are incredibly serious, and I can tell they think before they speak. When I talk, Dr. Huddleston listens and takes in every word.

August 26. Day four. It's been ten days since the last time I could eat and not get sick. I'm trying, but I just can't eat. Jen, one of my nurses, sits beside me in my bed to talk. They must get some nourishment in me because I cannot eat on my own. They are going to put in a feeding tube. Jen shows me this long, small tube, explaining that it will go through my nose and down my throat.

I have no words for her. There seems to be no end in sight. I already have IVs in my hands and one in my neck. I am too weak to carry on a conversation; I want to help, but I can't. All I can do is comply with whatever they want me to do with no complaints or arguments.

As they put the feeding tube in, it strangles me, taking my breath. They go fast, but it seems like a mile of tubing is shoved up my nose. It gags me as it goes down the back of my throat to my stomach. It is awful, and the last bit of strength inside me seems to leave.

I close my eyes and pray that everything they are doing will work.

With all this equipment hooked up to me—IVs, heart-monitoring wires, and the feeding tube—getting out of bed is a major undertaking. This is bad. I need to poop; they gave me some medicine to make this happen, but how am I to manage this? For the love of God, I don't know how to do this on my own.

My mom and dad have been living in my room.

"Mom, I need your help. I have to poop," I say.

She jumps up as the nurse says, "Oh, Jimmy, I can help you."

"No way. Mom, you help me," I say.

Mom pulls the curtains around my bed and helps me get on a portable potty on wheels. She helps me get situated, but I am so weak that even sitting up is difficult. I lean forward, and she holds me.

"Mom, why is this happening to me?" I ask.

She has tears now.

"I don't know, Jimmy, but God has got you in his hands, and everything will be all right," she says.

I know she is right. God is in this room with me.

That will be the only time I ask. God is the only one that knows. I just need an attitude of grace.

Mike, I love this guy. And he loves me. The world needs more Mikes.

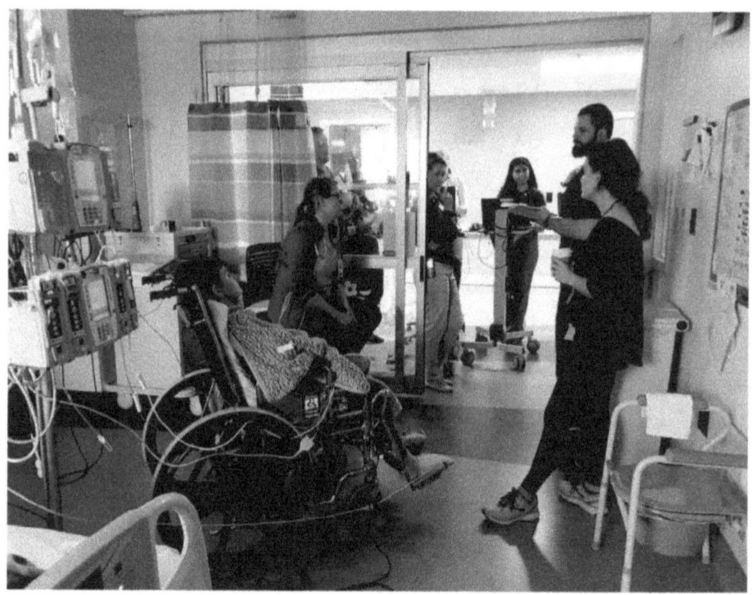

In a Bad Spot

—∾—

Today my nurse is Bri. She is a tall blond lady who, like Mary Grace, seems to be great at her job. There is no guesswork around here; everything is discussed, and the IV rack behind my bed holds no fewer than a dozen bags of drugs. The computer is programmed to alarm the staff if my blood pressure gets too low or my heart rate gets too high. The IVs beep when they need to be changed—it's nonstop. Bri has come early and has been arranging and rearranging IVs all morning.

At 1:30 p.m., the doors to my room are thrown open, and the glass walls are shoved back. Alarms go crazy, and people rush into my room. Some of these people are doctors and nurses that I have seen before, and some I don't recognize. My parents jump up from where they have been sitting.

My heart is beating fast—way too fast. Two hundred fifty beats per minute, and I can feel it. As the carts are shoved into the room, someone begins sticking pads on my chest. I see a cart holding the equipment they use to shock your heart. Voices are talking loudly; Bri stands over me, and she is calm. She talks to me in a normal voice, asking me how I feel; she looks me right in the eye, and I look straight into hers. We are both remarkably calm as I describe how I feel; yes, I know my heart is beating very fast. There is a man's voice I can hear over everyone else's.

"Who did that?" he asks.

"I did," Bri responds, still calm.

Everyone can see on the monitor that my heart rate is coming down. Bri has been putting a drug into my IV line during our conversation. Throughout the entire ordeal, she never takes her eyes away from mine. She monitors how I react to the drug as it goes through the IV.

Calm takes over the room. Crisis averted. My heart rate comes down, and the alarms go silent.

The crowd of people leaves the room, and the walls are put back in place. That's when I notice my dad standing next to Dr. Andreone, the older lady doctor who seems to live here. They stand just inside the room as she explains my blood pressure is too low and heart rate too high. Whatever they do to help one hurts the other; they are running out of options. She is nervous.

Dr. Huddleston has been called to my room. He and Dr. Andreone stand next to each other as he tells her he wants an arterial line. Constant blood pressure monitoring. No waiting for the cuff to inflate.

"No sedation. None. Can't risk it," he says.

Within a few minutes, a male doctor from anesthesia comes in the room; he is young, maybe thirty-five. He talks to Dr. Huddleston about the line and is quickly told I can't be sedated.

He looks at me, then at Dr. Andreone, and back at Dr. Huddleston.

"Well, I have never done that with a child. Adult, maybe, but never a child. Who is going to hold him down while I do it?" the young doctor asks.

"I don't think that will be necessary. Jimmy is not your average child. You explain to him exactly what you need to do. We won't have to get anyone to hold him down," Dr. Huddleston replies.

The young doctor comes to the side of my bed to explain the procedure. He shows me a small razor knife and explains he will need to cut me on the wrist. Then he shows me a long wire he will need to run up inside my arm in an artery so they can get a constant blood pressure reading.

Dr. Huddleston is still standing beside Dr. Andreone; my parents are just a couple of feet away. After a deep breath, I slowly lay out my left arm to the young doctor. I look him in the eye and tell him it's OK. As he begins to cut my wrist, he looks at me.

"OK, just please don't move," he says.

He cuts the inside of my wrist, takes the wire, and starts pushing it up in my arm. The pain is extreme, but I know not to flinch. Tears run down the side of my face. I don't want to cry in front of Dr. Huddleston, but I can't stop the tears from forming. It's done, and as the young doctor leaves the room, he stops by Dr. Huddleston.

"Well, I have never seen that before. That kid sure has an amazing attitude," he says.

"Yes, he does—the best," Dr. Huddleston replies.

After the doctors leave the room, my nurse looks over at my dad.

"In sports a great attitude can be the difference between winning and losing. In the PICU, it can be the difference between life and death," she says.

For the rest of the day and night, Dr. Andreone stands outside my room. The monitors say I am in reasonably stable condition, but she doesn't like what she sees; I can tell. There have been many conversations between the nurses and doctors about "studying the patient." The equipment is great; it all helps. Still, study the patient. How they look, act, and feel.

I hear her tell my dad that we are walking a fine line, and she is nervous.

Day five. It's been a long night. The tachycardia event from yesterday has taken its toll on me, and I am exhausted.

First thing in the morning, a small group of doctors and nurses has assembled in my room. One of the lady doctors sits on my bed, holding my hand.

"So, Jimmy, how do you think things are going so far?" she asks.

"Not good," I reply.

"Jimmy, if the medicines are not working to make you better, what do you think we need to do next?" she asks.

"Phase two," I reply.

Silence takes over the room as the doctors and nurses all look at each other, shocked at my answer.

"Can you explain to me what phase two is?" she asks.

Looking her in the eye, I take my finger, place it on the top of my chest, and run it down to my stomach.

"LVAD surgery," I reply.

Again, she looks around the room, then back at me with a smile.

They are shocked that I know what phase two is. All those mornings and evenings listening to the surgeons making the rounds, I have heard them discuss phase two and the need for an LVAD. I don't know what an LVAD is, but I know they will have to cut me open.

For the next hour, we sit looking through some books so I can understand exactly what they need to do to install the LVAD (left ventricular assist device): a pump to help my heart circulate blood. They will cut my chest open, stop my heart from beating, and sew a pump into the left side of my heart. Once they start the pump, the hope is that the right side of my heart will be able to do its job with no help.

An LVAD is a life-support device. It's not a permanent solution, only a temporary one. One of the nurses who comes into the room is Erin. This lady has the same energy as nine-year-old me. She is thin, about my mom's age, and always upbeat. She is the transplant coordinator.

She explains that it's time to put my name on the heart transplant list. It's hard to imagine hearing those words out loud. Three weeks ago I was in Orlando holding my trophy at the World Championships. Today I am preparing for a life-support device and the heart transplant list.

Erin now sits with my parents, discussing the process. I watch my parents, looking for signs of stress and trying to get a feel for just how scared I should be.

Mom has some tears, but moms are supposed to cry; it's just what they do.

To get a sense of how serious this is, I study the expression on my dad's face. I can see it locked away inside him. His ten-year-old boy needs a heart transplant to live. I have no words. I want to comfort him and let him know I will be OK, but I just pray for grace. God's grace comforts me; I pray it comforts him too. He goes for a walk.

When we first came to the hospital, no one thought we would be staying, so we didn't pack anything. Mom convinces my dad to get some air and take the truck back home to Jackson, about one hundred miles away. He can get some clothes for them both; a few hours in the truck will do him good, and she could use some one-on-one time with me. He reluctantly agrees.

Dad has been gone an hour or so when I start feeling faint, like I am falling into a hole. Alarms go off, and once again, the SWAT team of doctors and nurses storms my room. This time my blood pressure has dropped dangerously low.

Dr. Andreone is by my side. I hear "ECMO" but can't believe this is happening. ECMO is a life-support machine; if I am put on that, there is no turning back, no getting out of this hospital. It's a big machine that will act as my heart until a new one becomes available. They head toward my room. Another drug goes into one of the IV lines.

It works again, and my blood pressure comes up. My mom has been alone for this one; she stands by the small bed in my room, trembling. Tears run down her face as she calls my dad to get back quickly.

He will never leave again; she will never ask him to.

Phase Two

—~—

Morning comes, and I feel anxious. Dad has me at the doorway for the 6:00 a.m. meeting with the surgeons. My LVAD surgery will take most of the day tomorrow. Ashley and Whitney have arrived from Tennessee. Having my sisters here makes me feel better. Our room in the PICU stays full of people. I assume always having two nurses in my room must be normal. Later I figure out how unusual it is. Like I said, they take no chances here, and I am living on a thin line.

Molly from the life-care specialists department has become a daily visitor. She sits with me, and we attempt to play a game. She is a super fun and nice person. She is tall with red hair and is about the age of my sisters. Together they keep my mind off the surgery by playing games and telling stories.

Thor, the therapy dog, shows up at my door. Thor is a black lab, about the calmest dog you have ever seen. Amy is Thor's handler; as she comes into the room and leads Thor to the side of my bed, she tells us about the new dog therapy program. Thor is in training but has never actually been with a patient before. He lays his head on my bed to be petted, and we are instant friends. We will spend hours together over the coming months. When I frequent the hospital years from now, Thor will always remember me when I see him. When your life is full of stress, there is nothing like a dog.

Day seven. Surgery time. My sisters come early. The room is filled with staff: the doctors who will put me to sleep and the nurses who will be in the operating room. Dr. Huddleston comes and talks to us about the surgery and lets us know it will take most of the day. Hopefully the LVAD will relieve the stress on my heart and let it heal. It's possible that my heart can heal and a transplant won't be necessary.

My family and a group of nurses are with me as they push my bed down the hall. All I care about at the moment is making sure they have me asleep before they start. All night I thought about waking up in the middle of the surgery. The door closing is the last thing I remember.

For the next six hours, my family and a group of friends wait. Mary Grace comes to them regularly, explaining what is going on in the operating room and that I am doing great.

The surgery goes without a problem. God holds Dr. Huddleston's hand just like Dad holds mine.

—∾—

I don't wake up until 2:00 a.m. the next morning. Never have I felt anything like this. There is a breathing tube going down my throat and machines everywhere. Talking is impossible; my chest aches, and I can't move.

My eyes look to the bed where my parents sleep, and Dad looks at me. He gets up, comes to the side of my bed, and tells me everything is good. The surgery went perfectly. Dad asks if I'm OK, but there is no way I can talk; my arms feel heavy. So, I give him a thumbs-up and look toward the TV on the wall. Dad understands, turns on the TV, and finds ESPN.

Sometimes I need to not think. ESPN is perfect for that.

Losing track of day and night is an awful feeling, like losing your balance. I am too weak to talk, and I lose track of time. Not knowing if it's day or night, Monday, or Thursday is disorienting and unbearable. My sister Whitney puts a dry-erase board in my hand. It's my only hope at this point to communicate, but I can't hold my arm up long enough to write, and she can't understand as I try to whisper "time." I get the *T* written on the board, and Whitney sees my frustration.

She finally bursts out, "Time! You want to know what time it is!"

I nod my head yes. Losing track of time is awful; knowing what day and time it is helps me focus.

—ᴥ—

It's been two days since the surgery, and they are finally taking out the breathing tube. The pain is constant. There are staples in my chest and more IVs. I haven't eaten solid food for two weeks.

Tubes come out of my chest to a bag hanging by my bed. Bloody liquid drains through the tubes into the bags. Another tube comes out of my lower side. This tube has wires that go from the pump in my heart out through my side to a control module. For now, it stays plugged into the electrical outlet in the wall. There is a battery pack that I can later use to get mobile again.

The pain is intense; my heart doesn't beat anymore. The pump does most of the work for the left side of my heart, and I have almost no pulse; if you listen to my heart, you hear the swishing sound of the motor.

I have never felt thirstier. Mom gets me some Sprite, but swallowing hurts like crazy. Having a breathing tube for two days has made my throat feel raw and swallowing difficult, but I am so dang thirsty I just keep trying anyway. I am still nauseous; will I ever feel good again? It seems like no matter what we do, everything just continues to get worse. Talking is possible, but again, my throat doesn't want me to. As I lay my head back and look up at the white ceiling, Dad puts his hand on my shoulder.

"Hey, champ, I know it's bad, but we just have to stay focused on the big picture. You're in good hands; things are going to get better," he says.

My room is now full of gifts, cards, and posters. People have been bringing me stuff every day, but I have not felt good enough to look at most of it. Every time I throw up, my chest hurts so bad that I want to cry. Open-heart surgery is no joke. Cutting through the skin is just the beginning; they must saw my chest open to get to my heart. Right now, I can't imagine it will ever stop hurting. Someone has sent a teddy bear; I can see it on a shelf right next to a poster. Who would send me a teddy bear? Seriously, I am ten years old; I don't need a teddy bear! As I start to throw up, my nurse grabs the teddy bear and puts it against my chest. She tells me to press it tight against my chest anytime I need to cough, sneeze, or throw up. She's right; it helps. Whoever sent me the teddy bear, thanks.

Dad tells me that Coach Berube from the St. Louis Blues is headed to my room, and he's bringing the Stanley Cup.

I am seriously about to freak out. Here? Now? The pain is gone as a group of men come into the room carrying the real thing. The trophy is huge. Coach Berube comes up to my bed and shakes my hand as another man carries the trophy, placing it right up on the bed beside me. For the next few minutes, life is really good. Just for a few minutes.

The afternoon comes, and the pain and nausea take over. Alarms go crazy—another tachycardia. How is that possible? The doors swing open, and the nurse SWAT team is by my side. Two hundred fifty beats per minute. My heart is still weak, but once again, they get my heart rate under control. It's going to be a long night.

The veins in my hands and arms are now exhausted. There is a line in my neck, but the nurse needs to add an IV, and the last place available is my feet. She has my foot in her hands, rubbing along the arch area before looking at the top of my foot. She apologizes to me; she knows this is difficult and doesn't want to be the source of more pain. We have no options.

"It's fine," I tell her.

I wonder how I will walk with an IV in my foot; they say I need to get out of the room and try to walk down the hallway today.

With a small army of support staff, I get up. Someone pulls a pole with IV fluids while someone else carries the

LVAD control box. Mary Grace holds me up and down the hallway we go. Nurses and doctors make their way in and out of rooms and up and down the hallway, encouraging me. Walking fifty feet down the hallway is a major victory. I'm done for the night.

We have all heard that God never gives us more than we can handle. Well, God must think a lot of me.

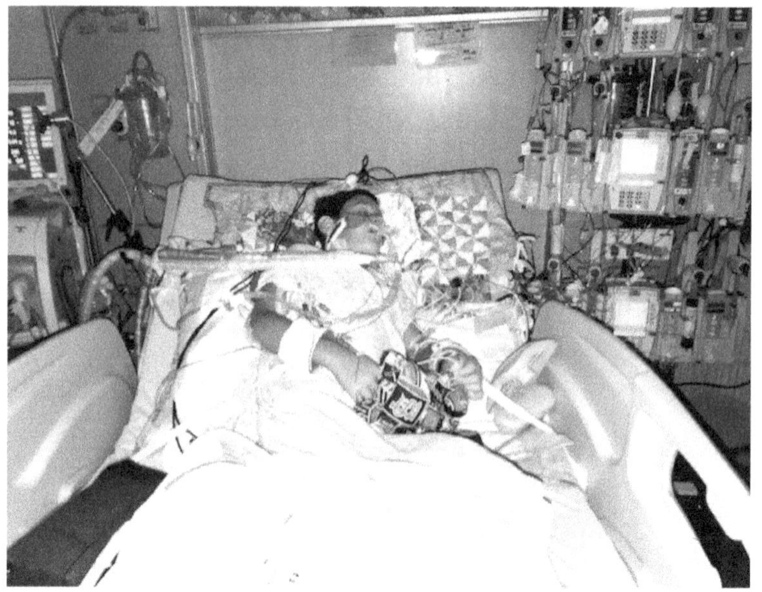

After the LVAD surgery.

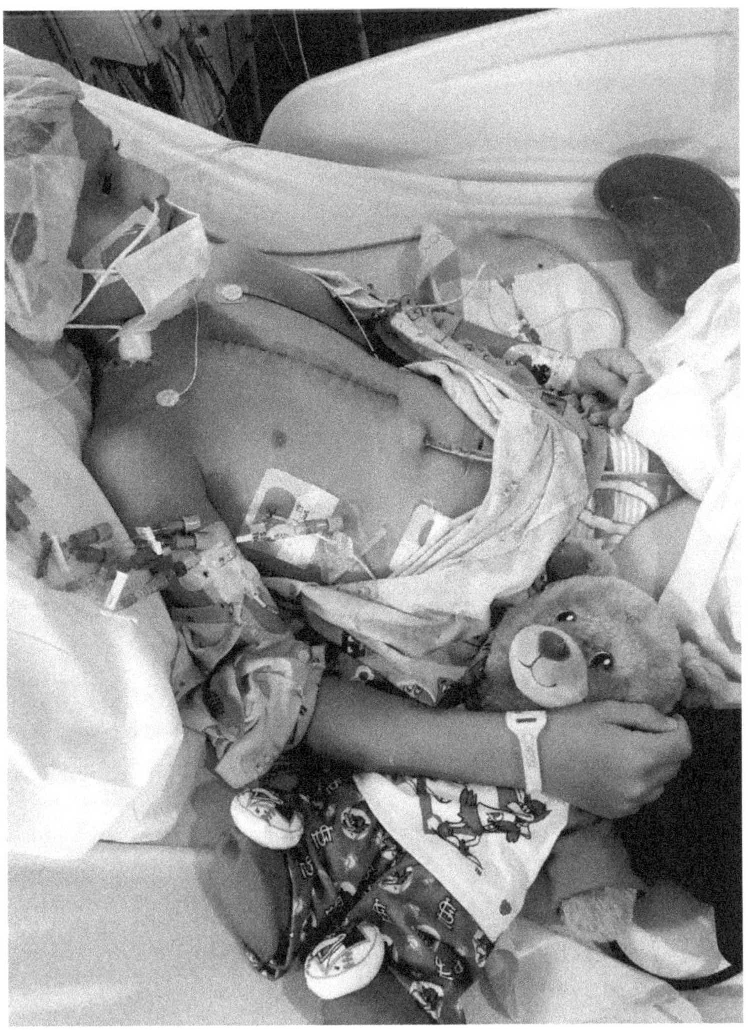

I don't think I ever felt worse than the first days after getting the LVAD

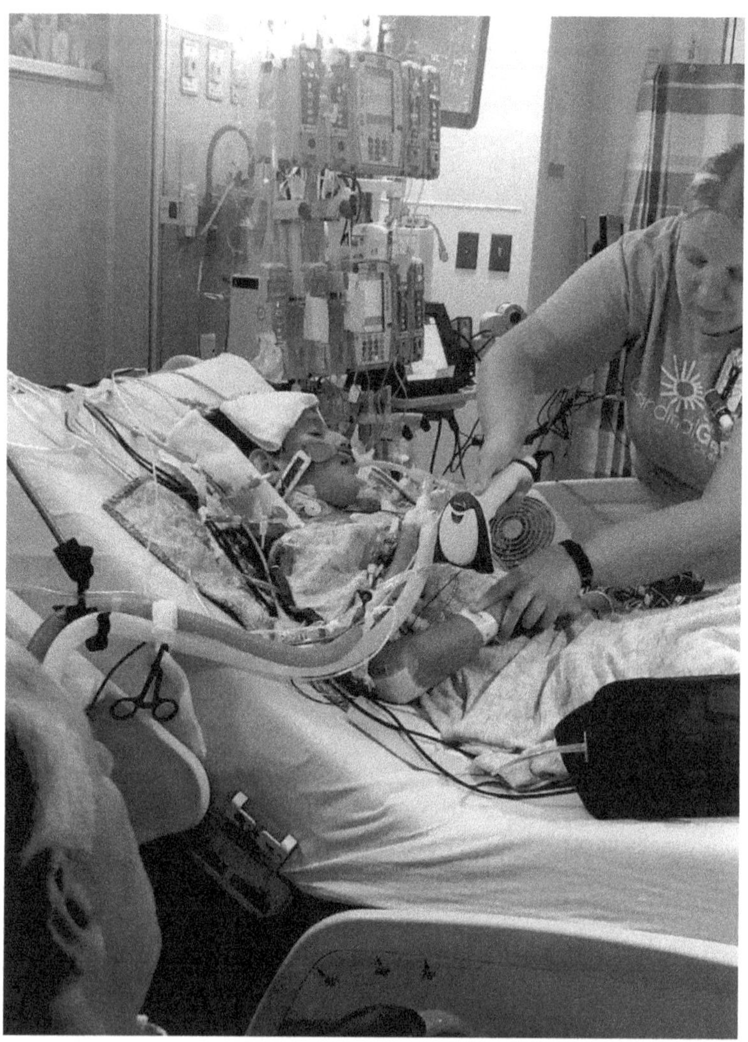

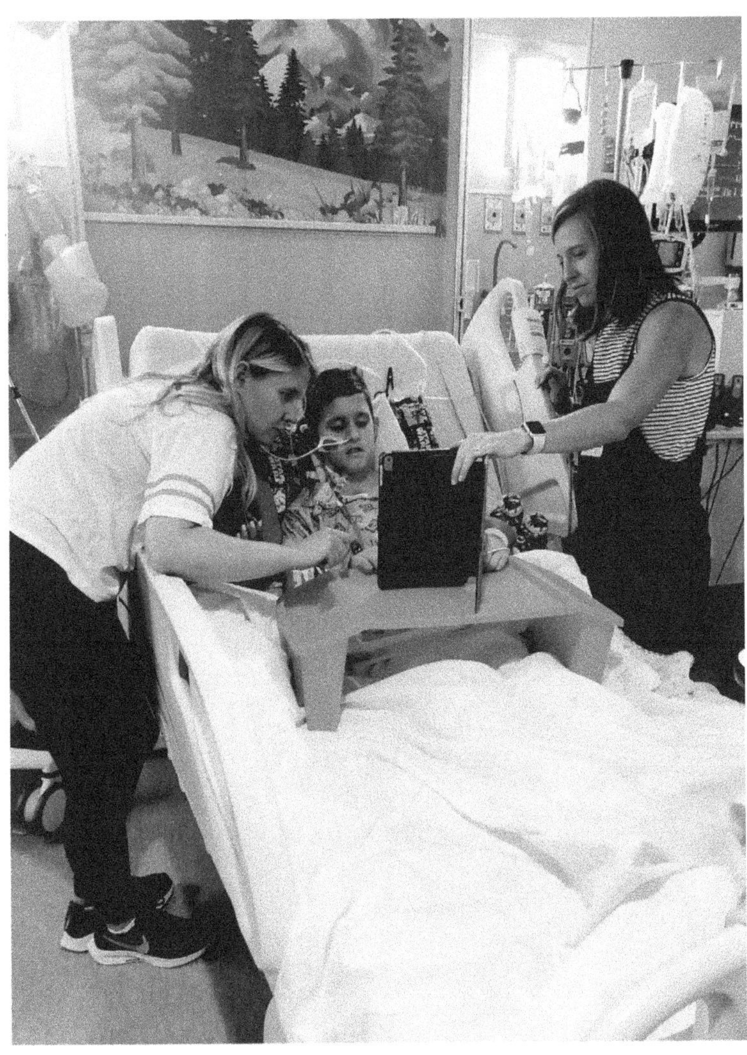

My incredible sisters, they live 400 miles away, have kids to take care of, but they seemed to always be with me.

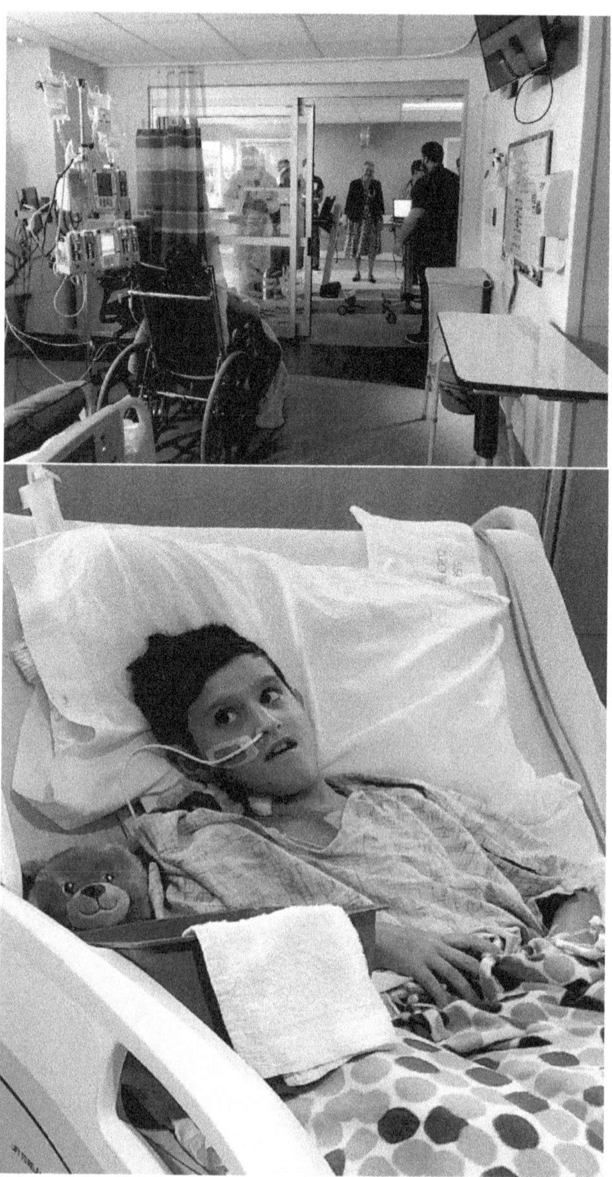

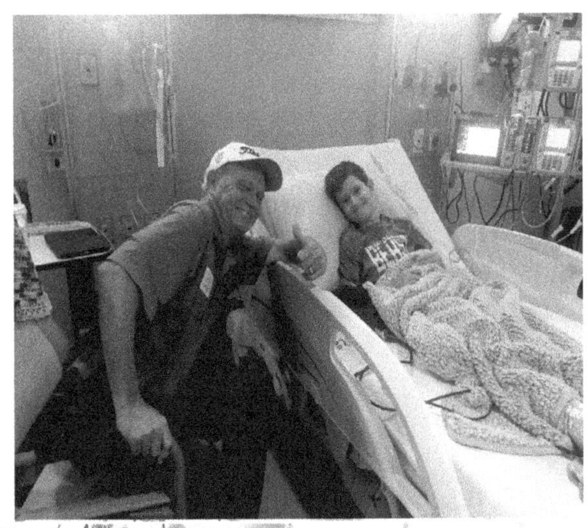

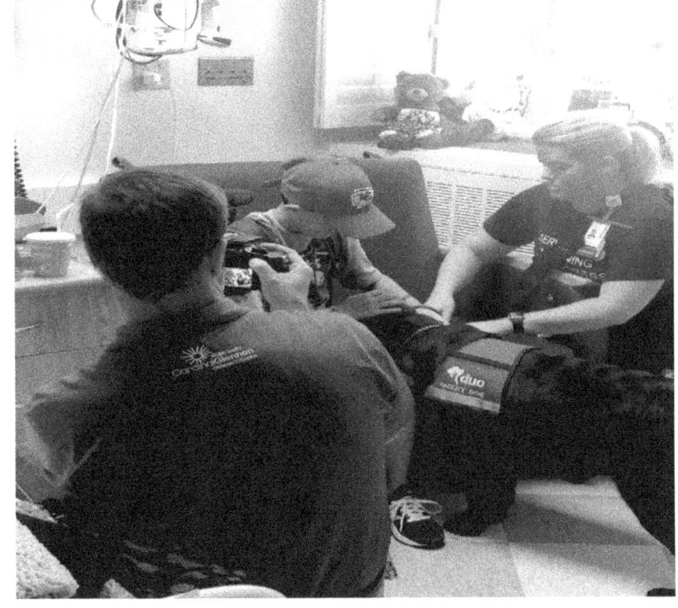

Thor, I was his first patient

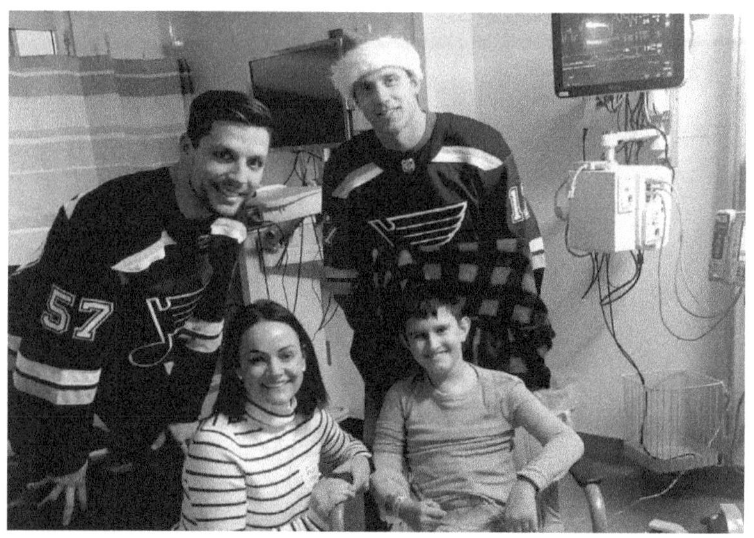
57

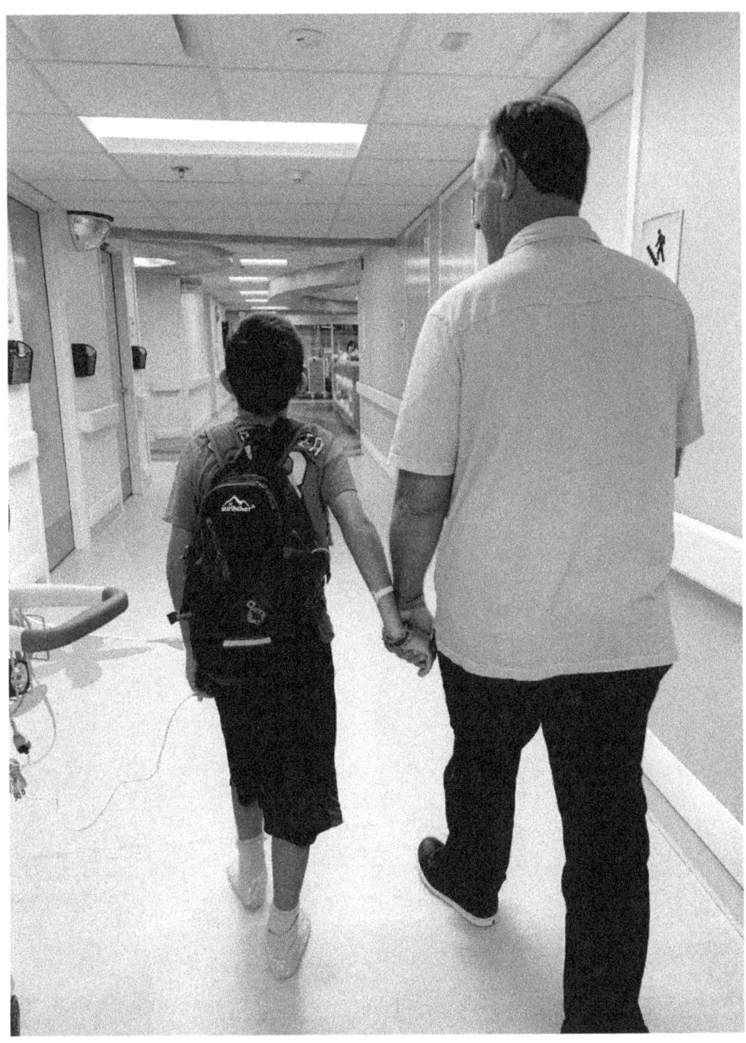

Dad and I walking laps. The control unit for the LVAD in my backpack.

Nurses Are Special

My nurse for the day, Keri, smells like pumpkin spice. She reminds me of my sister Ashley: shoulder-length brown hair, an olive complexion, and soft-spoken nature. As she moves around me, I smell pumpkin spice.

Today is maybe 10 percent better than yesterday, and any progress is welcomed. I know that I have had some of the best nurses taking care of me that anyone could hope to have. Mary Grace is a machine, constantly moving, directing, and getting things done. She has been as good to me as anyone could possibly be. She stops by Chick-fil-A to get me nuggets because she knows they're my favorite and purchases video games to bring to my room, even when she isn't my nurse for the day.

Bri is a real professional; she has saved my life, and I will never forget it. Bri will later transfer into the cath lab, where she coordinates my biopsies; when I go to recovery, she relieves the nurse from duty and takes over when she should be done and going home. I have wondered why she does that, and the best answer I can come up with is that she is special.

Jen spends many days and nights with me and has me stick her with the needle. She feels so bad about all the IV needles I am getting and the number of pokes it takes each time that she has me stick her. Sometimes to appreciate the patient's pain, you need a ten-year-old kid with a needle in their hand. Jen is fun—caring and fun.

Have you ever met someone and known right away that you could be real friends? Someone you could talk to about anything, and if you said it's a secret, they would honor it? For me, that's Keri. She immediately becomes my special person; I love her like family.

Throughout this ordeal I have stayed focused, knowing the only thing I can do to help is always have a positive attitude. Never complain about anything. Smile as much as possible. Keri deserves that from me too. I never want to make her job more difficult than it already is, but I can also tell her how I feel.

Sometimes I'm scared. Talking to Keri helps me get refocused. I can feel her Christian heart, and it comforts me.

Mary Grace. She was with me and my family from day one. She is a very special person.

Keri. I love her

Bri, she saved my life.

Brook and Keri

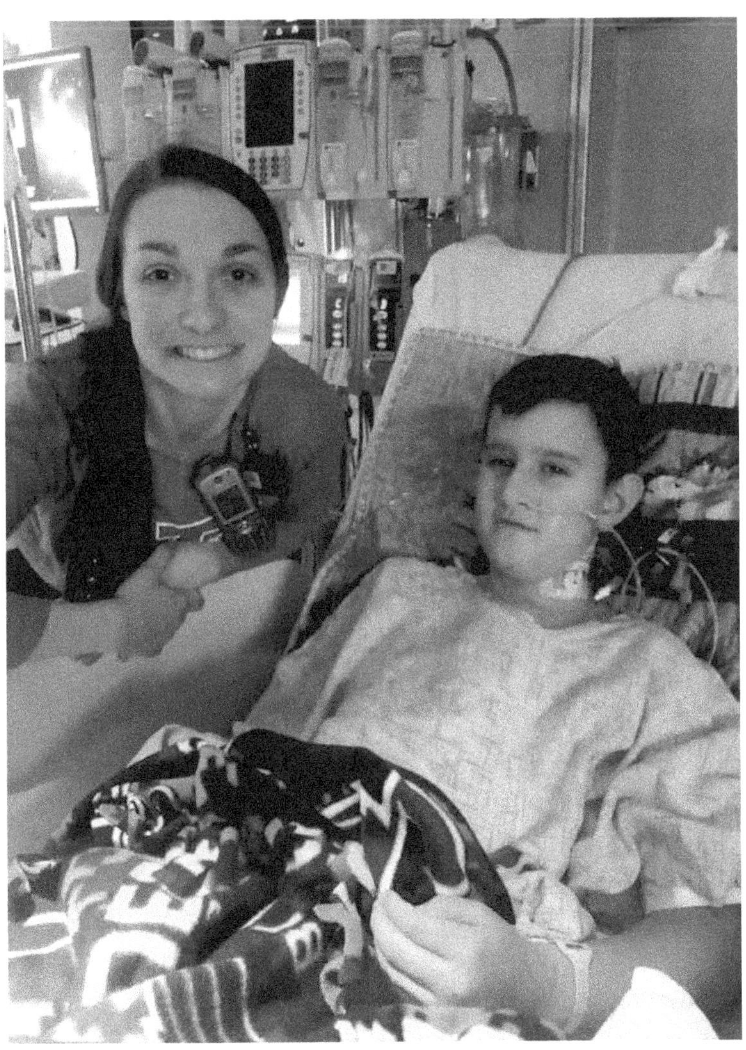

Jen

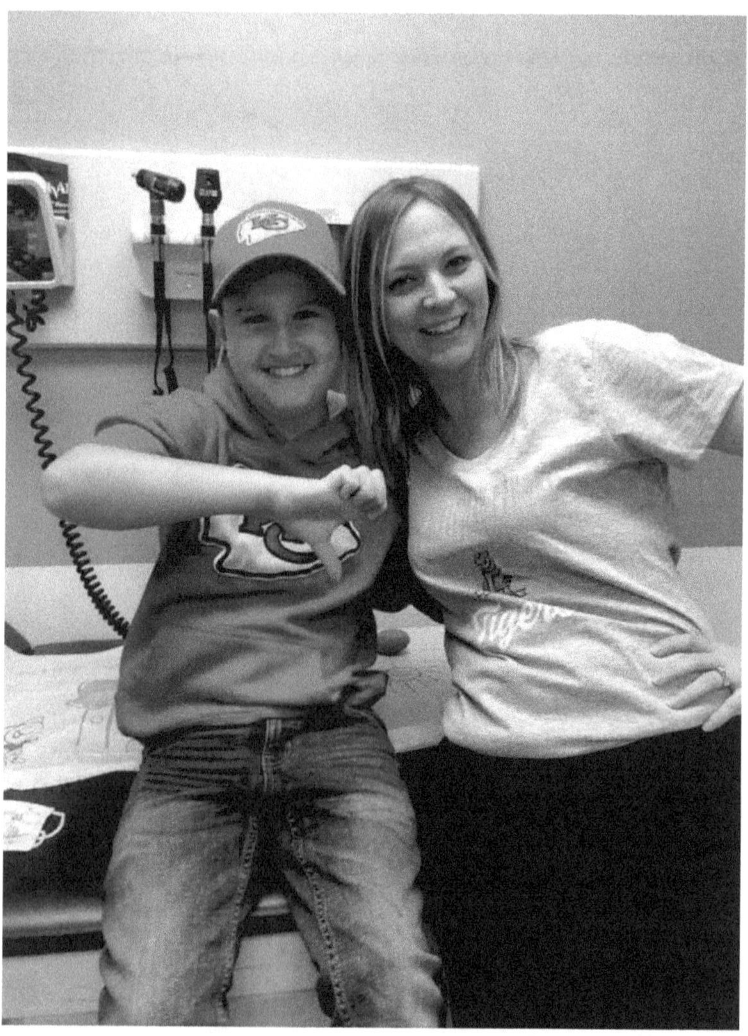

Always having fun with Erin..she is the Transplant Coordinator. I think my mom calls her every day.

Molly with Child Life Services. The work she does inspired me to start a toy drive. Over a thousand toys delivered so far.

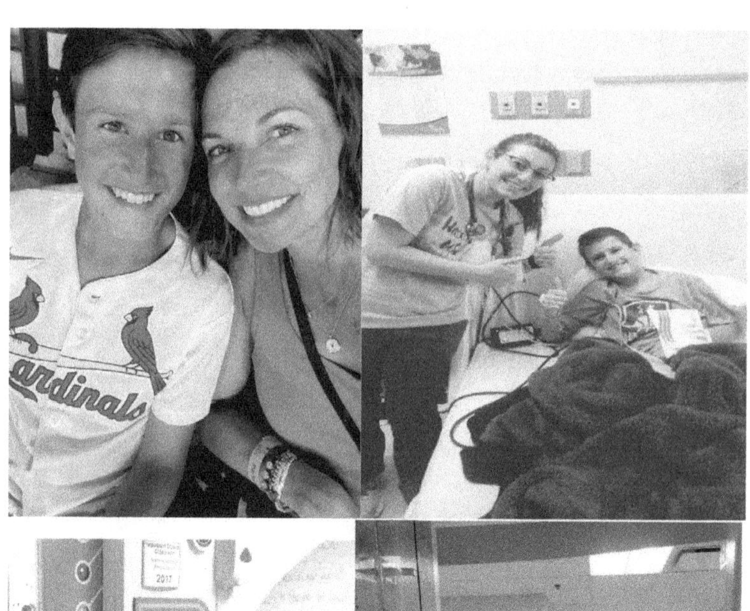
Cardinals

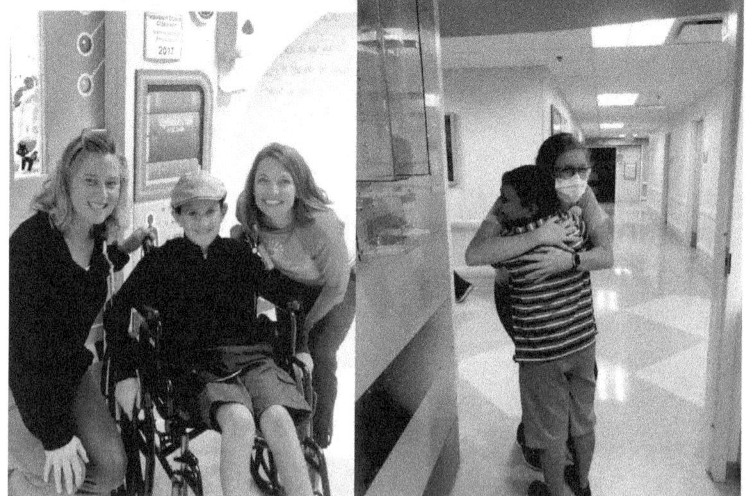

Birthday Breakout

—ɤɤ—

As the days pass since getting the LVAD, I start schoolwork again. Shelley is the teacher here, and she comes to my room for about an hour a day. Getting too far behind with school would be a disaster. Grades are a priority and always have been.

I've been running a low-grade fever for days. Today they are giving me a blood transfusion because I have become anemic.

If there is good news today, it's that I can eat; I actually feel hungry.

Dad rushes out of the room like a kid at an amusement park. He heads to the cafeteria and gift shop. He takes pictures of everything with his phone—candy, chips, and fruit. He brings me his phone, so I can look through the pictures and pick out something that I would like. Together we have a snack fest.

The new blood helps. I'm gaining some energy; I can feel it inside. The fever is gone.

Dad has me in my wheelchair and at the front door waiting for morning rounds. We have all gotten to know each other pretty well by now, and I have some suggestions.

Bath time should be in the evening; it wears me down and makes doing physical therapy difficult. We should do chest X-rays and labs a little earlier, before the schoolteacher arrives. All I get is smiles from the attending physicians.

"OK, Jimmy, sounds like a plan. Consider it done," they say.

—⁓—

Two weeks have passed since my surgery, and I have been in the ICU for twenty-two days. It seems like six months. I had hoped the LVAD would get me released from the hospital. Unfortunately, when Dr. Huddleston was working on my heart, he found scar tissue—lots of scar tissue. Going home is just not going to happen.

IVs have been coming out daily, and the feeding tube has been gone for a week. Eating is still a big problem, but at least I am eating. Protein is what I need. Lots of protein.

Amber is one of the doctors in the PICU. She is really young and totally jacked—a real fitness nut. She never ever leaves the PICU; she is here twenty-four hours a day, every day. I have often been on a walk and seen her at her station with her head laid down on the desktop. She also goes by her first name—the only doctor in the world that does that. She has been bringing me these little bottles of liquid protein, and they are stacking up because they taste disgusting, but Amber has a plan. My sisters are here again from Tennessee, so Amber gets a whole group of nurses together to come to my room. My sister Ashley finds a song on her phone where everyone is screaming, "*Shots! Shots! Shots!*" Amber, my sisters, all the nurses, and I all do a protein shot. Somehow Amber makes something as awful as drinking those protein bottles fun.

—∾—

Mom and Dad have been working out a plan with the doctors to get me out of the hospital. Home is ninety-eight miles from the hospital; there is no way they will allow me to be that far away with an LVAD sewn into my heart. Mom has found an apartment just a couple blocks away, the Metropolitan Flats.

Mom tells me the big news, and it's the happiest I have felt in months.

My birthday is coming up, and I won't have to spend it in the PICU.

Infection is one of the biggest concerns in any hospital

and is certainly a major issue for me. I basically have an open wound, where the lines from the LVAD come out my side, that is looked at and changed at least daily. Blood work is done every morning, but with my veins so exhausted, we have been trying to get the blood from my fingertips. They stick me and squeeze enough blood to fill a small vial and take it to the lab. The mechanical motor sewn into my heart with my blood running through it is working, but there are still worries. If my blood gets too thick, it could clot and jam up the motor; if it gets too thin, I could bleed to death. Great discussions for a ten-year-old to have, but it's my life. They call this my INR level: too high and too low are bad. So far, it's been good.

Me and my parents have started LVAD training: how to change batteries and what the different alarms coming from it can mean. My mom is trained to change the bandages and cover the area on my side so I can shower. All the area's EMTs get trained on the LVAD so that if there is an emergency, they are aware they probably won't feel a pulse or hear a heartbeat.

On September 23, exactly one month from the day I walked into the hospital, we walk out the same doors I walked in. Climbing into the back seat of our car and driving out of the circular driveway is a huge relief.

We arrive at the apartment building after a roughly

three-minute drive. Everything is busy around this downtown area. Forest Park is just a couple of blocks away in one direction; Busch Stadium, where the Cardinals play, is about a mile or so in the other direction.

We enter through the main doors to an awesome lobby area with big leather couches and a giant TV on the wall, a kitchen area, and even a workout room. Not much chance of using the workout area, but I see a shuffleboard, and as soon as I can get some energy, I want to take a crack at it.

Up the elevator to the second floor, we enter what will be our new home. It's great; as I walk in, I see big glass windows along the far wall that look out on the city streets and tall ceilings where I can see the ductwork. They call these kinds of apartments "lofts." Mom has been busy getting the place furnished, and my room is great. There is lots of sports stuff in my room, KC Chiefs stuff laid out on my bed, a TV and an Xbox all hooked up and ready to go, and my own bathroom. My first thought about my new surroundings is that they're easygoing. The natural light coming through the windows is so much different from the lights from the ceiling in a hospital room. Everything just seems comfortable. My first move is to find the couch; I'm worn out and settle in for a long nap.

Sleeping in a real bed feels great, but my mom and dad constantly enter my room during the night to make sure the LVAD is plugged into the wall outlet; the battery life is about eight hours, which makes them nervous. Showering in the morning is an adventure. Mom has half my body in Saran Wrap. She is scared to death that I might get the incision area wet, her hands shake as she changes my bandages. Part of me wants to say, "Oh good Lord, Mom, chill out," but I feel bad for her.

"It's going to be fine, Mom; we got this," I say.

I have Fruity Pebbles for breakfast, and I feel pretty good. We get the battery pack and control module loaded into a backpack, and we are out the door at 7:30 a.m., heading back to Cardinal Glennon for blood work. We log in on a screen in the lab, and they call my name. Two different girls working in the lab draw blood all day every day. Both are really funny and great at hitting a vein. They never miss getting a vein every time on the first try. Over the years, I will have blood draws hundreds of times at different clinics and hospitals, and these two ladies are the best of the best. No one else can ever get my veins on the first try.

Once blood draws are done, we grab the elevator to the second floor to see my teacher, Shelley, in the Shining Star schoolroom. This becomes my daily routine: blood work and an hour of school. Having just an hour of school sounds good, but I would give anything to be in school with all my friends.

We arrive back at the apartment at about 10:30 a.m., and Dad is waiting in the lobby.

"Jimmy, we have a phone call coming in about five minutes," he says.

We sit down, my dad's cell phone rings, and he hands me the phone. He tells me it's Todd Lewis from the Golf Channel, and I grab the phone. For the next twenty minutes, I am on the phone with Todd. He asks about my golf game and tells me stories about different PGA players and Tiger Woods. The whole time I just can't believe I'm talking to Todd Lewis. While I was in the hospital, Todd made a video of him at his announcers' booth wishing me well from all the people at the Golf Channel. They also sent me a gym bag full of the coolest stuff; it made me feel special, and I just kept asking my dad how Todd Lewis knew who I was.

People are so much better than the world gives them credit for. My room is so full of things sent to me from the Chiefs, Blues, Cardinals, my golf community at Kimbeland, and Dalhousie. There are letters from kids at my school—some I know and a lot I don't. They make videos at an assembly, wishing me all the best. I could never have imagined so many people really caring.

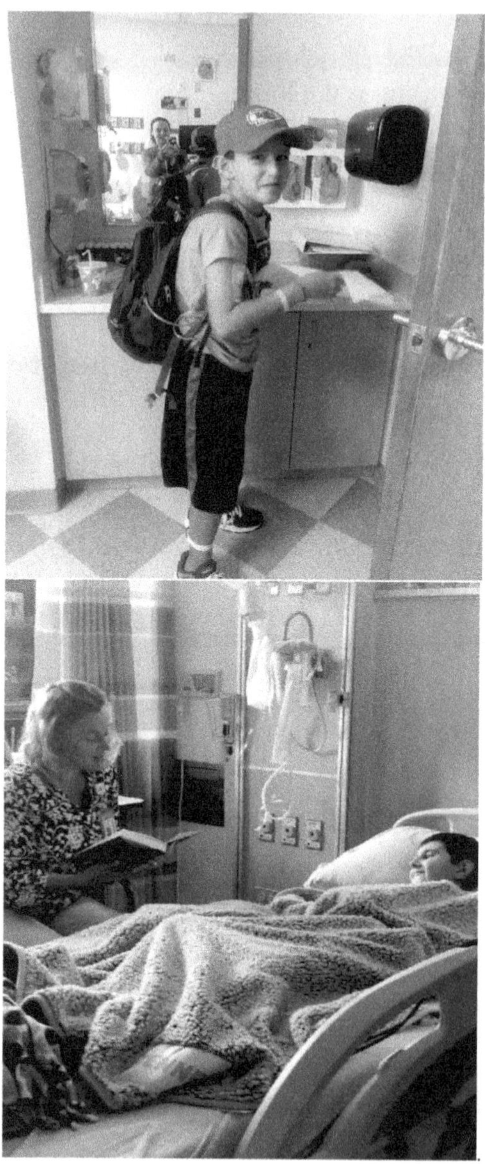

These ladies are the best. They have drawn my blood probably 100 times and NEVER have they had to stick me twice.

Love them.

First day at the apartment. I was exhausted by the time we got there. Being out of the hospital was incredible and in no time, it felt like home.

Todd from the Glennon Foundation. Lots of interviews and video as they documented my journey. You can see the video if you google "jimmy williams Glennon kid".

Once out of the hospital we started exploring the Central West End area of downtown St Louis. This was my first day out, I needed a wheelchair as I couldn't walk far. We treated this tense and stressful time like an adventure.

I soon became a regular at local golf courses putting with my LVAD control in my backpack

Lots of well wishes and visitors

Having family my sisters and Jack made everything better

We chose to be happy. Everyday we were greatfull to be together. Mom and dad and me.

Cardinals Baseball

MORNING COMES, AND I AM back for blood work and school. Shortly after we get back to the apartment, Mom's cell phone rings. My INR level is too low. Mom talks to Erin, the transplant coordinator, and they put me back in the hospital. Seems like we can't catch a break. I am out of the hospital for two days and now right back in—for how long, I don't know.

All the nurses and doctors in the PICU are like friends to me by now, so the thought of having to go back so soon is not great but not terrible. Then I get checked in and realize I am going to a regular room, in an area where I don't know anyone. I am not happy. Once I get settled in my room, a nurse is there to start the IV. She tries several times to get a vein but has no luck; digging with a needle is the worst. We calmly debate the situation. I make a point that I will get stuck less getting a shot every eight hours than with the unsuccessful IV attempts. As I make my point, a familiar voice speaks from the doorway.

"He is right; he will get stuck less. Let's just schedule him a dose every eight hours," Dr. Huddleston says.

As he talks, he enters the room and stands beside my bed. He looks at the nurse.

"Jimmy is a pretty smart kid and has certainly learned a lot," he says.

When Dr. Huddleston speaks, everyone listens. He's never loud or mean, but you can tell he's always right.

I immediately feel protected, like I got my people around here. No matter where you put me, they are coming to check on me and make sure everything goes right.

Within a few minutes Keri comes walking into my room. She is on her lunch break from the PICU and has come to check on me. There is a constant parade of nurses and doctors just coming by to say hello and make sure I'm OK.

—ııı—

After his evening rounds, Dr. Huddleston shows up again in my room. He has heard that I am just a few days from my birthday, and he knows I love the Cardinals, so he wants to make a deal. If we get this INR level up by tomorrow, he will take me to a Cardinals game.

To say I am excited is a major understatement. Bring on the needles—whatever we got to do.

Morning comes, and the lab results came back decent—good enough to get me released. We pack up and head to the apartment.

Game time can't come fast enough. I am waiting in the lobby with my backpack strapped on as Dr. Huddleston pulls up in front of our building; my parents and I jump in, and we're headed to the game.

The Cardinals are in contention for the playoffs. We need a win, and I can feel the excitement. Earlier that morning, I was weighed at the hospital and finally broke the sixty-pound barrier. My stomach will be healing for a long time, so nutrition is still a major concern.

Dr. Huddleston asks, "Jimmy, how about a hot dog?"

I certainly don't want to disappoint him, so I smile at him and say, "Well, sure."

The hot dogs at the ballpark are great, but they are also huge—there is no way I can eat that whole thing. I work on it but don't get a lot eaten before I slide it under my seat.

Somehow Dr. Huddleston has also arranged for Fredbird, the Cardinals mascot, to come to my seat between innings. I feel a little embarrassed by the attention but even more grateful. There are doctors, and then there is Dr. Huddleston. That day he not only makes me feel special but also gives my parents some confidence that I can get out and do a few things. Dad starts taking me to the games, nervous something will happen, but we continue going. The Cardinals win every game we attend and make it to the playoffs.

The following morning, we made our first trip to Chick-fil-A. Just a short walk from our apartment to the St. Louis School of Pharmacy, and there it is—my favorite place to eat. We begin making this trip every single day.

Shortly after returning and taking my twelve pills, which happens twice a day, Dad's phone rings. As he gets off the phone, he lets me know I have a visitor today. Jay Delsing, a PGA veteran who played on the tour for twenty-five years, lives in St. Louis.

Jay walks in the front door of our building as I sit in the lobby waiting for him. He looks more like an NBA player than a golfer; he is so tall at six foot five. Jay has the biggest smile on his face, almost as big as mine. He is the same age as my dad but with a lot more hair—gray hair but a lot of it. We sit in the lobby and talk for a long time. At first, I want to be nervous. I have never met a real pro golfer, but we have great chemistry, and he becomes a real friend. Jay will be a regular visitor for the remainder of my time in St. Louis. He meets us for lunch and invites me to come to Norwood Hills Country Club for a putting contest. He takes me out on the course to chip around while telling me stories of Ben Hogan winning a tournament there. I want so bad to be able to really swing a golf club that day, to show him that I can play, but the pain in my chest from the pump and the ten-pound weight of batteries in my backpack make it impossible. But it is a great day. Life is certainly not all bad.

As the days go by, my strength continues to get better. Every day I have blood work and school. More visitors come. Ozzie Smith, the greatest shortstop of all time, comes to see me. We have a crowd that day. My parents, grandma, and Mom's friend Beth are all huge Ozzie fans. The banter between him and me is awesome. We joke and laugh, talking about sports, baseball, and golf.

Some of my friends from school are finally able to come and visit. Jack, the golf pro from Dalhousie, comes with the owner of our course, Cord Dombrowski. Drew, a fellow member, comes one day and brings me a bag full of stuff from Jackie Burke, the oldest living Masters champion. In the beginning I would wonder, why all these special visits? I really didn't get it. Why all the special attention?

—∾—

Life is as normal as possible, but the days turn into weeks. My sisters come regularly. Ashley brings my nephew, Jack, and we play all day. All these adults have been fine, but man, have I needed a kid. Liam, one of my best friends, starts coming regularly. We play in the apartment living room, throwing a football around and breaking a few things, and go to the zoo. I can tune out the seriousness of my condition and be me…just a kid.

Our routine is in place; we go to Cardinal Glennon Children's Hospital every morning. Mom stops at the Starbucks coffee stand as we head to the elevator; she is like best friends with the lady that works there. I seem to know everyone in the hospital, and after class, it sometimes takes an hour to leave as we stop and visit with nurses, doctors, and staff. When given the opportunity, I always stop by the PICU and say hello. There is always a pain in my chest from the pump. Some days it's worse than others, but I never let on about it. Smiling and talking about normal stuff masks everything.

Our family time in the apartment is calm and comforting; we are all thankful to be together. No one seems stressed, but I know deep down they are. Every time my mom's phone rings, she jumps. If it's a 314 area code, she heads to her bedroom to take the call. Is this it? Is this the call?

Interviews with Todd from the Glennon Foundation continue. Sometimes they have a film crew at the hospital. They occasionally come to the apartment or have the film crew follow us on walks around downtown.

Dr Huddleston and me at the game

Top: Jay Delsing

Bottom: Ozzie Smith

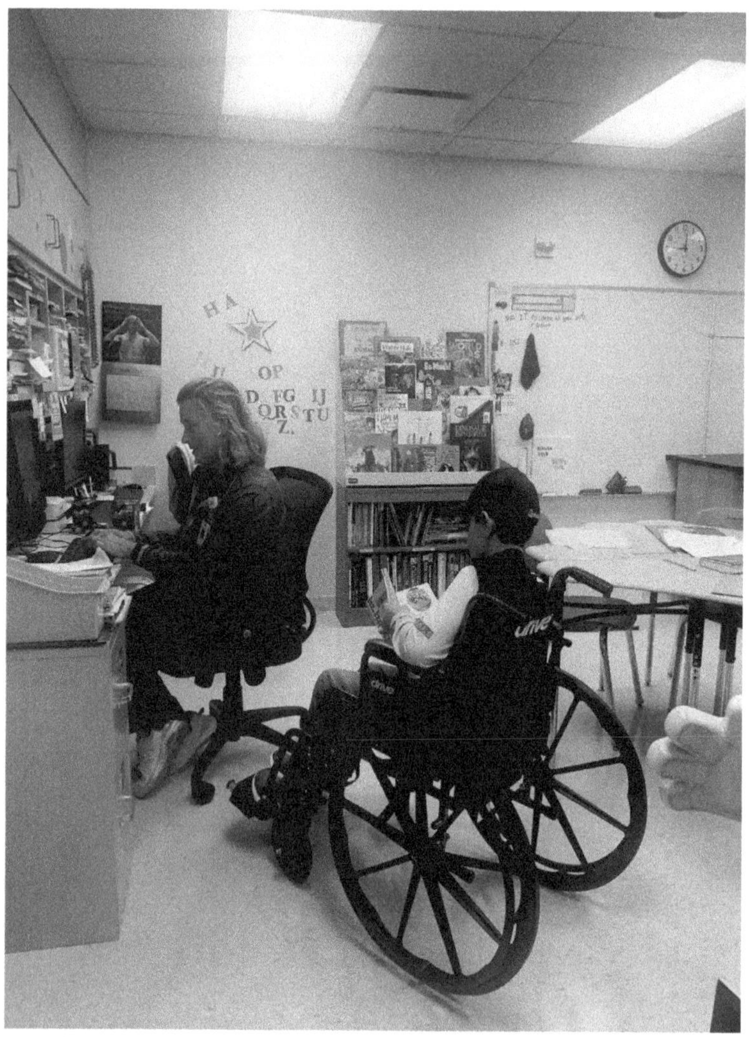

Shelley with the Shining Star School at Cardinal Glennon

God Bless Christina

Wait for the Lord; be strong and take heart and wait for the Lord.
—Psalm 27:14

Mom loves every holiday! At home she has Christmas trees up all year long and redecorates them for every holiday—Christmas tree, Valentine's tree, and Easter tree—all year long. So, to make our apartment seem more like home, she puts up a tree, decorating it for Halloween. We are about to carve a pumpkin when the phone rings.

It is Mom's sister-in-law from Chattanooga. My story of an eleven-year-old boy waiting for a heart has spread through Facebook, family, and friends. A teenage girl in Chattanooga has been in an awful car wreck; she will not survive, and the family will donate her organs. Her mother knows of me through her church; her daughter has my blood type, B-positive, and wants to donate her daughter's heart to me directly. There are complicated criteria for getting on the transplant list, such as different levels of urgency and limitations on how far away they can travel to get a donated organ. The process begins. There are tests to be run and phone calls to make. Next to my door in my bedroom sits a black gym bag that stays packed and ready to go. For now, we wait for the doctors to review the tests and X-rays of the girl's heart. The transplant teams in Chattanooga are talking to our transplant team and many others.

Late that night our transplant coordinator calls to tell us that Dr. Huddleston and Dr. Fiore have decided to wait; this will not be my new heart. Mom has been a nervous wreck, in and out of her room a hundred times crying and praying for the donor's family. I don't know if I should be disappointed, but I remember Dr. Fiore telling us weeks ago that we will wait until we have the perfect heart—perfect for my size. Everything will be perfect. So I trust them, and I trust in God. There will be another one for me; this girl's heart will save another life.

For the most part, I feel better all the time. Some days the pain from the pump is worse than others, so some days are spent just hanging out in the apartment and playing video games. Thanksgiving is now approaching. I haven't seen home in months, and although I have had lots of visitors, I want to see home. Thanksgiving dinner should be at Grandma's house. Smelling the food cooking in her house is like nothing else in the world; I just feel at home.

I decide to take matters into my own hands and start negotiating. I talk to my cardiologist Dr. Schowengerdt during a regular checkup; I tell him I want to go home for Thanksgiving badly. He promises that if all my blood work and echoes look good, I can go home for one day.

So down the hall we go to see Mike. I jump on the table, he starts the echo reading, and we talk some serious smack.

The echo is finished, and everything looks good. I slide off the table, swing my shirt around above my head, and dance. Going to Jackson! I am so excited.

Early the following morning, we get our things together. Mom goes to take some things down to the parking garage underneath the apartment building. She isn't gone but a few minutes before walking back in the door, crying. Dad walks over to her to find out what's wrong, but Mom keeps crying and finally explains that her car has been stolen—it's gone.

Dad hesitates for a second or two and bursts into laughter. Mom looks at him like he is crazy.

"Replacing a car is the least of our problems; I thought something really bad had happened," he says.

We all jump into Dad's truck and head to Jackson. It's about a hundred miles, and on the way, Mom explains that our first stop is Kimbeland Country Club for a reception and lunch. Jim Davey, our golf pro, has helped Mom arrange for a bunch of my friends and members from the club to gather for lunch there. Happy is an understatement! Getting to see friends and classmates after being gone for months? It's perfect.

After a couple of hours at the reception, I head out to the putting and chipping area to get some practice with my LVAD hanging in my backpack. Jim Davey comes with me. My first attempt is from about thirty feet. The weight of the backpack and wires coming out of my stomach make it difficult to have any sense of rhythm, but my first attempt is good. The ball checks up and is about four feet from the cup. I look back at Jim, standing there with his arms folded and a big smile on his face. We both know I still got it. I'll be back.

—∾—

The smell of food cooking at Grandma's house for Thanksgiving dinner is the best. Life just always feels right at Grandma's.

We leave Grandma's and go home. Sleeping in my own bed is good, but not getting to see my dog, Shep, is a real bummer. Ashley picked up Shep when I first got admitted to the hospital, and he has been staying with her in Tennessee.

Knowing that tomorrow morning we will head straight back to the apartment in St. Louis keeps the mood a little gloomy. Still, just being there gives me some additional hope that I will soon be back for good.

At Kimbeland CC with Golf Pro Jim Davey for our Thanksgiving visit.

Mom making every day fun

Why Spenser

—⁂—

"For I know the plans I have for you,"
declares the Lord, "plans to prosper
you and not to harm you, plans to
give you hope and a future."
—Jeremiah 29:11

MONTHS HAVE PASSED AND STILL no new heart. I cringe at the idea of praying for a heart, knowing what must happen for me to receive one. The thought of never getting one has started to creep in as I lie in bed. I trust God that everything will work out. I have faith.

Our routine of blood draws, waiting for the call that my INR levels are fine, echoes, and chest X-rays continues.

Life in the apartment is comfortable; we have made it

home. We are happy and thankful to be together. At night, Mom wraps me in plastic for a shower, changes my bandages, helps me get situated in bed, and plugs my LVAD control box into the electrical outlet. Somehow, we have been able to make all that seem normal.

—⁓—

December 11. I have been looking forward to today; Dad and I are headed to meet Jay Delsing for lunch. Jay has friends on the St. Louis Blues team and has managed to get a ring, the one they got for winning the Stanley Cup. He is bringing it with him, and I get to hold it.

Jay arrives just as Dad and I get seated in a booth. I slide over to sit with Jay, and he immediately opens the box and takes out a ring that's the size of my fist. He takes my hand and slides the ring on my finger. Dad is taking our picture just as his phone starts to ring.

Mom is on the other end talking to Dad; he looks at me while talking to her.

"Oh my God, this is it?" asks Jay.

Dad nods yes and steps away to finish the call.

Minutes later he is back with the details. We have a heart. Tomorrow is the big day. We will check in at 10:00 a.m. tomorrow. I stare at a plate of Chinese noodles, trying to smile and be excited as emotions and thoughts race through my head. Just when you start to give up hope, it happens.

Thinking of what they must do to me is scary. For the second time, they will have to cut my chest wide open. This time they will have to take my heart out and put someone else's heart in.

Whose heart am I getting? What happened to them? All these thoughts race through my head as we drive back to the apartment.

When we get inside, I go to my room. I need a moment to myself to pray for myself and for a family I do not know.

Tomorrow has never seemed so close, and yet the waiting is hard. Shortly after dark, my sisters show up. They jumped in a car and drove from Knoxville the minute Dad called. No one feels like eating, and I can tell Mom and Dad are not about to go to sleep. I don't want to dwell on any of this, so I ask my mom to get me ready for bed. Tonight will be the last night with my LVAD. Mom wraps me up to cover the wound and stands just outside the shower curtain, holding the control box to the LVAD and keeping it away from the water as I shower. Then I crawl into bed, determined to get to sleep as fast as I can. It takes a while, but eventually, I drift off. I want to sleep, but I don't want to dream.

Morning comes, and everyone is still sitting in the family room. It looks like I am the only one who slept. No meds this morning, which by now seems odd. The medications thin my blood so it can run through the LVAD without clogging it up. Having thin blood and heading into surgery doesn't seem ideal, but I trust they know what they are doing.

As we arrive at the front of the hospital, the film crew is there taking video of me walking into the hospital and getting checked in. I am in a constant state of prayer, conversing with God in my head and asking him to help me, my parents, and all the doctors with what we all must do today. I pray I won't have a lot of pain and will remain completely asleep, not suddenly waking up in the operating room.

We get to the room in the PICU, and it's familiar territory—a constant parade of all the doctors and nurses who have been a part of my journey from the very first day. There is lots of hugging between everyone. Molly from child life services is there and stays with me all day. Within a few minutes, Thor the therapy dog walks in the door, and I immediately feel better. He is a load, but he gets up into the bed with me, lies down, and never leaves my side for the next five hours.

Everyone is really positive; there is a feeling of confidence that overtakes the room. It's standing room only. As the hours go by, I just focus on me and Thor, not thinking anymore about the surgery.

As 5:00 p.m. approaches, Dr. Fiore comes into the room.

He explains that Dr. Huddleston has flown to Illinois to retrieve the donor's heart from a hospital in Peoria and will bring it here. Dr. Fiore will be in the operating room with me, preparing me to receive my new heart. Erin, the transplant coordinator, will communicate the progress of my heart arriving at Cardinal Glennon Hospital. The final stages of removing my old heart and putting me on the heart and lung machine will not take place until Dr. Huddleston and my new heart are safely in the building.

Dr. Fiore takes my parents' hands, bows his head, and prays. He asks for God's help and guidance throughout the surgery. As I listen to him pray, I can feel his sincerity. It is a huge comfort to know that my entire surgical team—especially the doctor taking out my old, damaged heart and sewing in a new one—has asked God to help. We won't be alone in there; God will be with us.

The anesthesia has me feeling relaxed. Nurses are at both sides of my bed as we make our way down a hallway to the operating room. Before we go through the doors, I look at my mom and dad and give them a thumbs-up. It's game time.

Under normal circumstances, the surgery takes six to eight hours, which is what we expect.

When Dr. Huddleston arrives in Peoria, he is informed that a change has been made. The donor's liver was larger than they had anticipated, so now they have the chance to divide the liver and donate it to two babies, so there is a delay. Luckily for me, I am sound asleep in the operating room. There is plenty for Dr. Fiore to do before the new heart arrives. Hours are added to the process; it will be thirteen hours from the time they rolled me into the operating room till Erin calls my mom and says, "We have a heartbeat."

My family, sisters, parents, Grandma, and a small group of friends camp out all night. We received the call on the eleventh. It is now the thirteenth, and none of them have slept, just prayed. Erin calls my mom occasionally with updates, and Mary Grace sits with them off and on through the night.

Dr. Fiore makes his way to the waiting area to see my parents. The surgery is a success, and my new heart has picked back up, beating immediately. He says it was the most complex surgery he has ever been a part of in forty years. Scar tissue from my damaged heart and the LVAD made everything more difficult. In his matter-of-fact tone, Dr. Huddleston calls it a "perfect result in a complex situation." I call it a gift from God. The heart, this hospital, these nurses, and my chance to continue living are all gifts from God.

Later that morning I am moved from the recovery area back to my room in the PICU, where Jen, the nurse that let me stick her with a needle, waits for me. Mom and Dad are given a stethoscope and listen to my new heart.

Tubes are coming out of my body everywhere—two tubes from my abdomen and two from my chest. A breathing tube is down my throat, and IVs are in my neck. As I start to finally come to, the pain is bad. Even with all the drugs, my chest is really hurting.

Then it happens again. The alarms blare. My blood pressure is dropping, my heart is beating fast, and I can hear Mom praying as they stick the pads to my chest in case they have to shock my heart.

The drugs work yet again, but this won't be the last time.

Dr. Fiore comes to check on me and is made aware of the issues. He sees the concern on my parents' faces and has the nurse remove the pads from my chest, explaining they will not be necessary.

The following day comes, and Mike, the echo man, is here to take some more movies of my heart. As he leaves, Jen brings me the stethoscope and puts it to my ears. I listen to my heartbeat. It seems bizarre as I realize the LVAD is gone. I have lived with it and that swishing sound in my chest for four months, and now it's gone; I have a heartbeat.

My first attempt to walk is forty-eight hours after surgery. The line in my neck and the two in my stomach are finally gone. Dad has my hand, and Jen pushes the IV pole, but I don't make it past the door. I want to; I want to show everyone I'm doing good and getting better, but my chest is killing me, and I just can't. Dad leans over and tells me, "It's fine, champ; we can try again tomorrow."

Having your chest cut open once is tough; having it cut open twice in a few months' time is more than twice as bad. I don't think I was really prepared for how much worse this would be than the first time.

New drugs—antirejection drugs—are pumped in. The nausea is constant; it's been three days, and it is time to try to eat some solid food. I order some pizza and tell Jen I'm ready to walk, so Jen takes my hand, Rachel takes the pole, and we start lapping the PICU. Three laps and I'm toast, but I have proved to myself I can do it. Pain, nausea—nothing can stop me now.

Every day that passes, I get stronger. Visitors are allowed now, and although it's always good to see Ashley and Whitney, I am getting some cool people. St. Louis Blues hockey players show up; they just come right in and sit down with me—it's amazing. Ryan O'Reilly hangs out one day, then Jaden Schwartz and David Perron the next. Pro golfer Jay Delsing comes with his girlfriend, Karen. When my friend from home Drew comes by, he jokes that I'm not as excited to see him as I should be; I quickly tell him who he's up against. While Drew is in the room, one of the nurses from therapy stops by. Her name is Molly, and she is one of the few nurses I have that's single and about the same age as

Drew. I immediately introduce them and try to get a date going, and they both turn solid red. I'm back; I can feel my swag. Smiles fill the room more and more. We may be stuck in this hospital, but we can still find something to laugh about.

Spenser, 11 years old.

His heart saved my life.

Someday we will have a lot to talk about.

Having lunch with PGA veteran Jay Delsing when we got THE call.

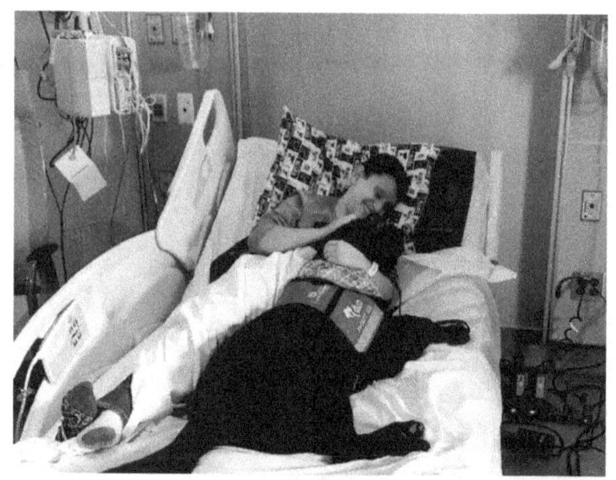

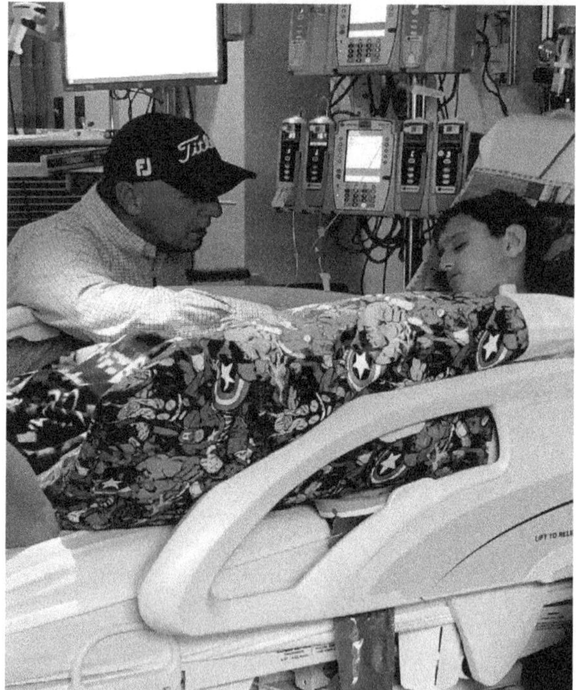

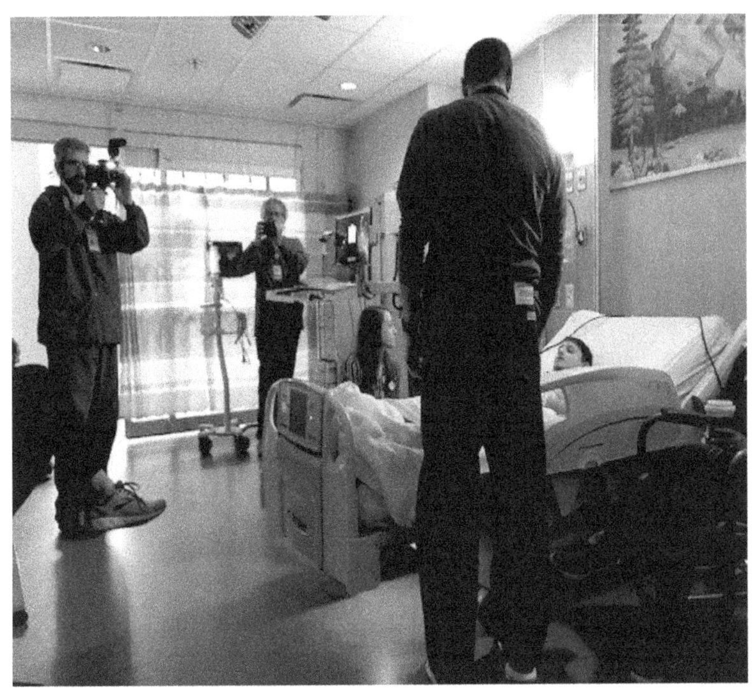

Dr Amber Alber sitting with me before my transplant. Todd and the film crew documenting they even came in to the operating room

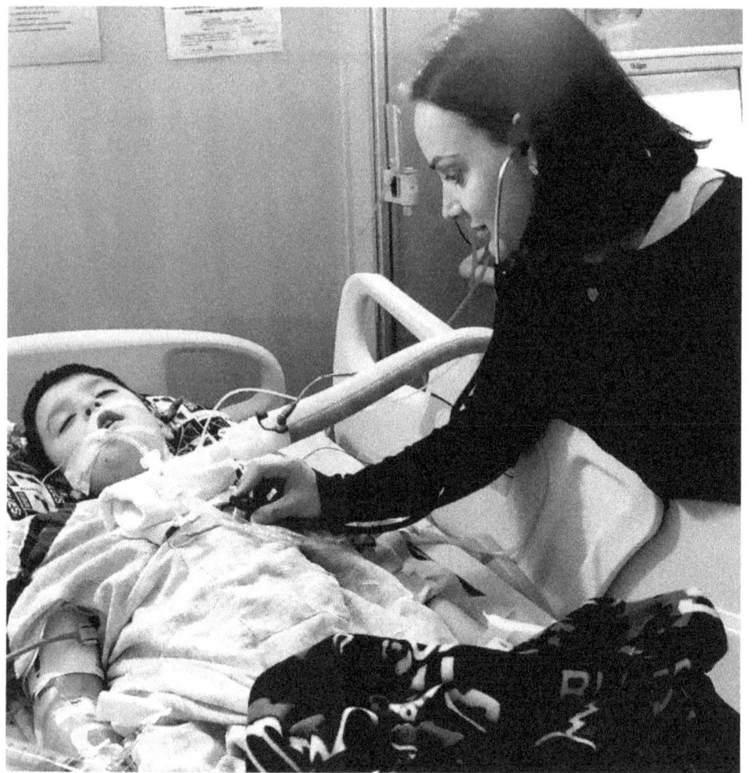

Mom listening to my new heart for the first time.

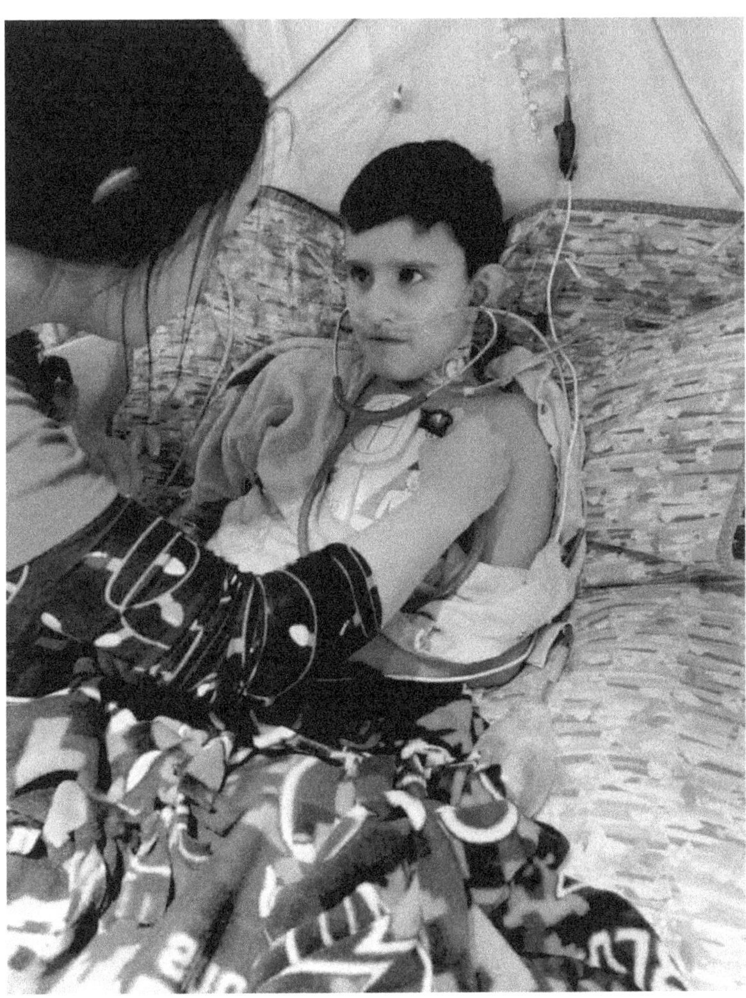

Jen was there when I woke up and let me hear my new heart. For months all I heard was the swishing sound of the LVAD

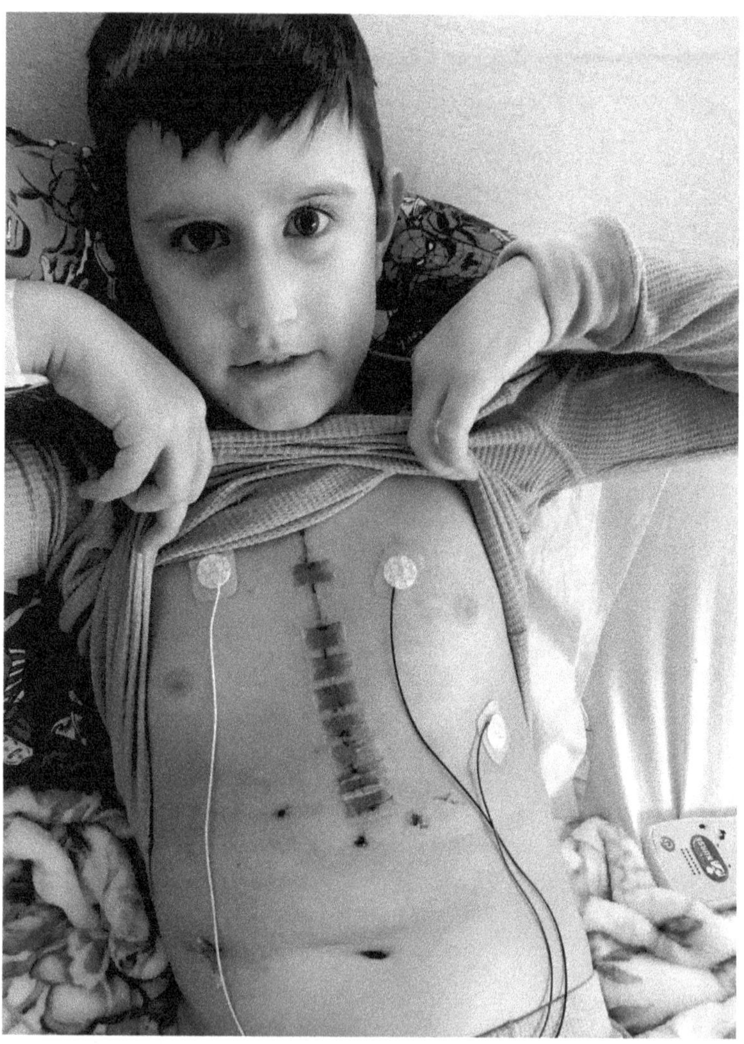

Greatest Christmas of My Life

CHRISTMAS IS FAST APPROACHING, AND we have all gotten comfortable knowing we will spend it in the hospital. Keri has arranged her schedule so that she can be my nurse the week of Christmas.

A lot of neat stuff happens around Cardinal Glennon for Christmas, like Light Up Glennon. The community comes at night to stand around the outside of the hospital and shine lights up at the windows while kids in their rooms shine lights back. Channel 5 News comes, and I get interviewed; it is my first time on TV.

Mom decorates our room with lights and a small tree. As we go to sleep on Christmas Eve, my parents on the pullout couch and me in my hospital bed, we are not sad that we are here. Our room is filled with happy and thankful thoughts. I tell my mom that this is my favorite Christmas—the absolute best of my life.

Christmas Day comes, and Keri and I get a football. We go outside and play catch. I'm sorry she is not with her family and tell her so, but I am sure thankful to have her here.

There have been so many changes in such a short time. To think of it all at once is just too much.

Living with a transplanted organ creates a whole new set of issues. The doctors tell us from the start that this is not really a cure; it is trading one disease for another. This new disease must be treated daily and monitored forever. For the rest of my life, I will take meds to keep my body from rejecting my new heart. Blood draws and biopsies make sure the meds are doing their job.

Today is my first day of training. Most of the medications so far have been through an IV, but I will take pills going home. Erin, our coordinator, brings a bag of pills into our room, and we go through them together. Mom is there, but they want me to be involved to know what each pill is and what it's for; I want to know too.

Erin empties the bag, and my eyes want to pop out of my head. There are so many pills that it's hard to imagine. Twenty-four pills a day. Twelve in the morning and twelve at night. We fill pill organizers for morning and night, seven days at a time. My parents get me a new iPhone so I can register what I have taken and when. I set the alarm for 7:00 a.m. and 7:00 p.m. because the timing is important too.

We have had discussions about life after the transplant, but it's starting to register that this never goes away.

The doctors want to do a biopsy of my new heart before discharging me, and the first available time on the schedule is the day after Christmas. They make an incision in my groin area and run a line up to my heart, where they take pictures and some small pieces from different areas of the heart. Those are run to the lab and tested for rejection.

Rejection occurs when the body's immune system attacks the tissue of the heart. They have me on drugs that lower my immune system to keep that from happening. None of that sounds very good, so I just take that information and log it in my brain. To dwell on it would serve no purpose other than making me sad, and I don't ever want to feel sad. Of all the things I have learned through this ordeal, the most important is to stay as positive as possible and be happy. It's a conscious decision and one I make throughout the day. As I hear troubling things or think disturbing thoughts, I just log the information I have to know, accept how I go about some things will be different, and then move on and find something to smile about.

Results from the biopsy come back, and there is no

rejection. The incision site hurts like crazy and only adds to the chest pain, but we are cleared to get out of the hospital.

Fourteen days after the surgery, we are out of the hospital and back in the apartment. Our routine here is comfortable; school at the hospital for an hour, blood work, and then freedom for the rest of the day.

The steroids (prednisone) make themselves known to my body. Eating and staying nourished has been a problem for so long that I have forgotten what real hunger felt like. It's back with a vengeance. Most mornings I have breakfast at the hospital cafeteria; I love their French toast and bacon. After school is out and we are back at the apartment, Dad walks me to the Chick-fil-A, and I eat again within the hour.

I gain ten pounds within no time, and my cheeks feel tight. At first, I am glad, and my parents are super happy, but it doesn't take long till we can all see where this is going.

I start hitting the gym in our apartment building every day for at least thirty minutes or so. Golf season is several months away, but I am anxious to start getting my body stronger.

New Year's Day comes, and it's a really nice day. The sun is shining, so I convince Dad to take me to the driving range at Forest Park, which is just a mile or so away. It's been eighteen days since my heart transplant, there are staples in my chest, and I am chipping balls on the range. Mom isn't crazy about us coming and makes me promise to just putt. After a dozen or so pitch shots, I am dying to see if I can get into one. As I look over at my dad, he can tell what I am thinking and says, "*No*, don't even think about it." He's right, but I sure want to.

Life is what you make of it, and we make the most of every day. School with Shelley is fun, and I like her a lot. She coordinates everything we do with my teachers back home, so I will be caught up when I return to school. I make As in all my classes.

We take walks around the downtown area daily and have plenty of visitors. Liam from my baseball team can come and stay with us on the weekends, and my sisters make the trip back and forth from Tennessee every few days.

Dad gets a call from the golf pro at St. Louis Country Club; they have invited me to their club if I am up to it. I immediately drag Dad to the truck. St. Louis CC is one sick place; the range is all I can attempt, but it has bent grass that looks too good to hit off.

Grant, the pro that invited us, gets me in the pro shop as we leave and gives me a gift bag with golf balls and a hat. Over all these months, I have constantly been amazed at how many people that don't know me try so hard to show me kindness. This world is full of great, kind, loving people who go out of their way to be nice to kids, especially kids in a hospital. I will be one of those people for the rest of my life.

My goal of going home to Jackson is within reach. If these next few echoes and blood draws are good, then all I will need is for the next biopsy to be clear of rejection.

At my doctor's appointment, the camera crew shoots some more video. They have asked my family to attend the Heart & Soul event in February to benefit the Dallas Heart Center. It's a big fancy affair with hundreds of people who raise money for kids like me. This video documenting my journey will be played there.

Jackson Tribe is the name of the travel baseball team I play on, and they have been selling shirts that say "Jimmy's Tribe" on them. A lot of people have bought them; kids at school, teachers, people around town, and even my nurses wear them. When we first find out what they are doing, my dad asks what I want to do with all that money. I tell him that giving it to child life services here in the hospital is a great thing to do. They have done everything possible to help me, playing games and bringing me things almost every day; I will feel great if I can help make that happen for some other kids.

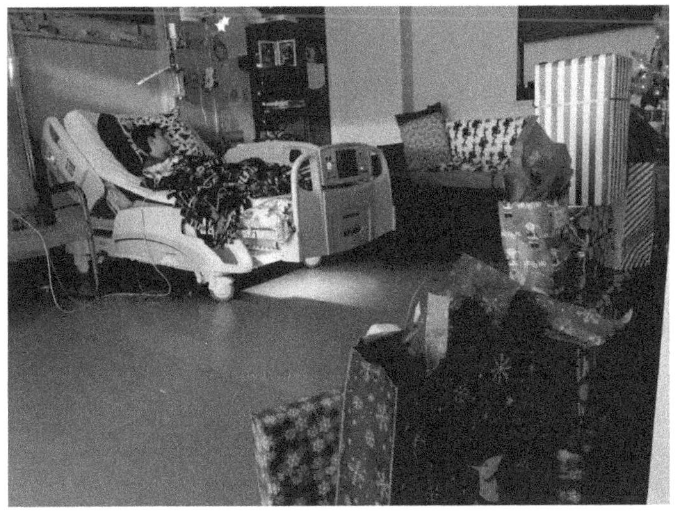

Christmas Eve.

Light Up Glennon, what a incredible thing for the community to do at Christmas

Christmas day

Going Home

—☙—

January 13. Thirty days after the surgery and it's time for another biopsy. With good results, I will be heading home. The last time, they went in through my groin; the incision kept me from hitting golf balls for a few days, so I talk to the doctor who does the procedure and ask if he has to go in there. He explains he can go in through my neck. Getting cut in the neck doesn't sound great, but I ask if we can try it.

The procedure only takes about an hour. It's done in the operating room, and they put me to sleep to do it, so there is not much stress on me. While looking at my heart, they notice one artery where they attached my heart is narrowing, so they do angioplasty to open it up. If that doesn't stay open, they will put in a stint next time.

Biopsy results come back the following day, and once again, there is no rejection. Mom dances around the apartment, and we start packing our bags. Going home—real home—brings feelings of happiness and relief. Finally, I will be at home for good. My dog, Shep, has been at my sister's for months, and I immediately start pleading with Dad to get my dog. I want everything back to normal.

As we pull into town, we drive by my school, and I can't believe my eyes. The street in front of the school is lined with kids and teachers, most wearing their red Jimmy's Tribe shirts and chanting, "Jimmy! Jimmy!" Mom cries and honks the horn while everyone waves.

What I wouldn't give to be back in school. For now they want me to stay home. I am recovering from the surgeries with a lowered immune system, so my best hope is to get back with my fifth-grade class for maybe the last month of school. Little do we know, something called COVID lurks in the distance.

Life takes on a more normal feel immediately after we get home. My school has a teacher, Ali, who comes to my house several times each week to help me keep up with schoolwork. Sitting down at the kitchen table with your teacher doing math might not sound like something a fifth grader would enjoy, but I do. Ali is cool to be around, and the one-on-one help makes the work easy.

Several days a week, I go to the gym and meet Drew, who helps me get in a workout. It's not a lot, but just being around someone other than my parents can be good, even if they're an adult.

Friends are able to stop by, and we go to the movies. Being in school would be better, but this is still good.

Trips to St. Louis are still weekly for checkups and echoes to make sure my heart is still acting right. On one trip I go by KLR 550 radio station for a live interview promoting the Heart & Soul Gala; I love doing that.

February 1. We are back in St. Louis for the Heart & Soul Gala at a big, fancy ballroom in a hotel downtown. Dad takes me to get a suit for the occasion; my sisters, Uncle Jamie, and Aunt Julie have flown in from Tennessee. Tonight, I will give a speech and present a check for $4,500 from Jimmy's Tribe. Mom will also give a speech, and she is so nervous she is sweating and is almost mad that I'm not nervous at all.

As we walk in, the ballroom is all lit up fancy. We find our table, and just as we sit down, Jay Delsing and his girlfriend, Karen, walk up. They sit with us at our table, and I am shocked. I have had the opportunity to meet many sports stars and some celebrities, but Jay is just different. The day we met at the apartment, I told my mom he was maybe the nicest person I had ever met. He has continuously gone out of his way to be a friend, and I will be forever thankful.

To get the evening started, my whole family is called

on stage, and they play a video on the huge screen above our heads. It's only a few minutes long, but it shows what our story with Cardinal Glennon has meant to us. After the video I get up to the podium and give my speech, thanking everyone at the hospital for saving my life. I present the check, printed on a huge sign so big that I need help holding it. All five hundred people stand up and applaud for several minutes.

Mom gives her speech and does good, but of course, she cries some. She just can't talk about me without crying.

Immediately after we return to our seats, they start an auction. All kinds of stuff is being sold. Dr. Huddleston keeps bidding on a package for Cardinals tickets and throwing out the first pitch. It goes for thousands. He gets it and says it's for me.

That night raises a few hundred thousand dollars, the most they have ever raised, and I want to believe I am at least a small part of that. I will do anything I can to help Cardinal Glennon Children's Hospital for the rest of my life.

Celebrating at the Heart and Soul Gala 2 months after the transplant.

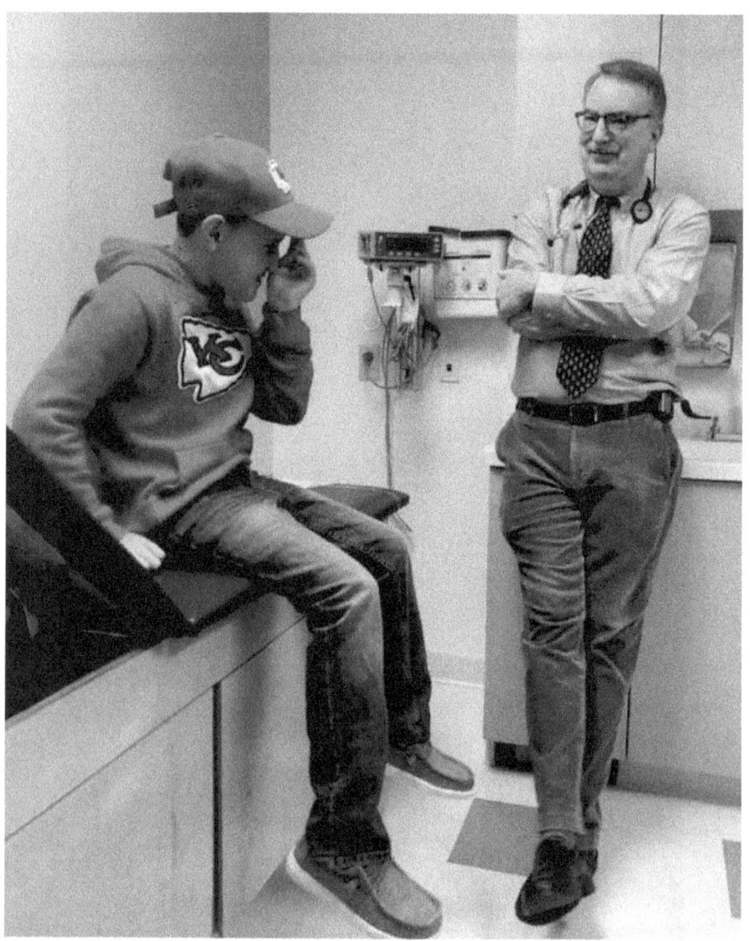

Dr S. releasing me to go home.

The Long Road Back

—⁓—

GOLF IS A BIG PART of my life, but I am not ready to give up on everything else. Football is a stretch because the doctors have advised against it; although they are not crazy about my playing baseball, they have not completely ruled it out. I have been working out at an indoor baseball facility to regain my form. Endurance is an issue, but I can make it through the hour-long practice.

Every day I get bigger—and I don't mean taller. When I look in the mirror, I don't recognize the face I see. The steroids are taking their toll; my face is getting rounder by the day, and I have probably gained twenty pounds in the last six weeks. It bothers me, but I don't know what I can do about it.

February 2 is an unusually warm day, so Dad loads up our clubs, and we head to Dalhousie.

Jack is waiting for us at the bag drop area, and I can tell he is fighting the urge to cry. Loading up our clubs and heading to the first tee box is an old familiar feeling and a welcome one.

Dad follows me to the tee box and stands behind me, filming with his phone. People say playing golf is nothing like riding a bike, but it is to me. I'm dead center down the middle of the fairway with a slight draw, and I hear Dad behind me saying, "I'll be. Right down the middle."

At first, we play five or six holes; every day the weather permits, we are on the course. Eventually, we play nine holes and then twelve. After a few months, we finally make all eighteen. It's a far cry from thirty-six holes plus hours on the range, but I'm making progress.

I have blood drawn once a week, regular visits to Cardinal Glennon for echoes, and biopsies every ninety days. The veins in my arms are still exhausted and difficult to stick, my feet hurt, and my strength is slow to improve.

COVID makes the national news, and there is no way I will be allowed to return to school this year. By the time school lets out for summer, I have only made it to one day of the fifth grade. Hopefully, I will get to go next year. If not, I will miss being in middle school entirely.

Gold Medals and Rejection

—∞—

May 28. Five months after the transplant, we drive to Dexter, Missouri, for the season's first tournament. On the ride there, I feel some nerves building up—not so much about how I will play but more about seeing all the players and them seeing me. I don't look like me.

Dexter is the first tournament every year, and every year it rains. Jack hands out the scorecards and pairings and, as always, holds a prayer before we head to the first tee. Mom and Dad grab a golf cart and follow along like always.

My nerves are gone. I tee up and send my first drive down the middle. My feet hurt, and the wet ground makes walking even more difficult, but I keep smiling and try to forget what hurts.

For the next few hours, I am really me again, talking football or Cardinals baseball as I walk between shots and congratulating the other players when they hit a good shot.

At the end of the round, we walk inside the clubhouse, turn in our scores to Jack, and eat some pizza while he gets all the boys' scores posted by their names. When he hands out the medals, he calls my name, "In first place, Jimmy Williams." I'm back.

June 2 is a win. June 15, another win. Three tournaments in a row—all wins.

The day after my third consecutive win, we get a call from Erin, our coordinator at Cardinal Glennon. The results from my latest biopsy show rejection. It's a word no transplant patient wants to hear, and for the first time, I drop my head and cry. More needles, even more weight gain from the steroids. Mom and Dad give me a few minutes to process it all. I get my game face on and tell my parents, "All right, let's do this."

After three days in the hospital getting pumped full of steroids, I start to look like the Pillsbury Doughboy.

The road back just got a little longer.

But here I am, thirteen years old. Sixteen pills a day, biopsies every six to twelve months.

I am back with my classmates after missing two years of school.

I work on my golf game almost every day. I am playing golf tournaments again. I have won a few, and I plan on winning a lot more.

Any day they could call and say I am in rejection.

Saint Peter writes that life will not defeat you if you keep an attitude of grace.

Positive and grateful people give thanks for everything in their lives, even on the days when nothing is going right.

That's my story: A story of adversity. A story of overcoming adversity. A story of grace.

I've learned so much about God's grace over the years. A positive attitude isn't just the key to winning golf tournaments; it's the key to a meaningful life.

And sometimes a positive attitude—an attitude of grace—is the difference between life and death.

I am grateful that my faith as a Christian is connected to God's grace and his unstoppable love for us.

Suffering is a part of all our stories. Name it. Stare it down. But don't dwell on it. When we're spinning out of control, God is still going to be God.

Be strong. Trust in the power of God's grace. Let Grace build a positive attitude within you.

At some point, your life will depend on it.

GOLF

Steroids can do some drastic things to your body. I didn't recognize myself in a mirror.

Left to right Dr. Huddleston, me, and Ed Hempstead Cardinal Glennon Board of Directors at Old Warson Country Club.

National

St. Louis

Meet my co-chair for Homers for Health. Cardinal Hall of Famer Matt Holliday

Nothing can replace golf. But I do love speaking and sharing how Gods Grace fills my life.

Dan Dierdorf

Erik Compton stopped in at Georgia Bulldogs Golf Camp to meet me. Erik is a PGA tour professional and has had not 1 but 2 heart transplants.

He was ranked as the Number 1 Amateur when recruited to Georgia and was a member of a National Championship team.

My friend Clay Yates. Clay had a heart transplant just a few months before me. Clay reached out to me shortly after I came home from the hospital. We have a unique and very close bond. Pictured here in San Diego for the Transplant Games where Clay and I brought home some gold medals in golf.

PXG

My family

JIMMYS
TOY
DRIVE

PLEDGE
FOR
PATIENTS
homersforhealth.org
SSMHealth
CardinalGlennon
Children's Hospital
HOMERS
FOR HEALTH
heartland
Cardinals
Cardinals

CPSIA information can be obtained
at www.ICGtesting.com
Printed in the USA
BVHW041657010223
657465BV00001BA/1

9 798986 541389